T0208792

The Tangled Web

A LITTLE GIRL'S STRUGGLE TO
OVERCOME RACISM AND POVERTY

FRANCES HEWLETT MORRIS

authorHOUSE

AuthorHouse™
1663 Liberty Drive
Bloomington, IN 47403
www.authorhouse.com
Phone: 1 (800) 839-8640

Published by AuthorHouse 06/29/2020

ISBN: 978-1-7283-6533-6 (sc)
ISBN: 978-1-7283-6532-9 (e)

Library of Congress Control Number: 2020911542

Print information available on the last page.

This book is printed on acid-free paper.

Contents

Dedication

This book is dedicated to my young granddaughter, Mya. When I was her age, I lived in a world that was confusing and difficult to understand. My family and I experienced racism and lived in poverty. She and other children are living in a similar world now.

Racism and poverty happen and children should know they exist. They see evidence of it with their own eyes. Children are not blind to race. They notice skin color and differences. There are people who have more money and there are people who have less money. Some people have darker skin and some have lighter skin. Some people have curly or coarse hair and some people have straight hair. These are differences that must be embraced. Children must learn that no one is more important than the other.

Children are smart and curious. As they try to understand the world around them, they learn what they live. They may have questions about race and poverty that are not answered by their parents. Maybe they don't know how to answer. If not answered, children come to their own conclusions and their conclusions may not be correct. They pay attention to who is around them and may tend to show preferences for people who look like them. Parents shouldn't remain silent. Avoiding talking about race and poverty will not make it go away.

Racism is a learned behavior and we owe it to our children to teach them it is wrong. Racism may lead to poverty because of the way people are treated. Children should know that racism and poverty do not only happen in history books. These are not easy topics to discuss. We owe it to our children to talk about these difficult subjects so they can understand.

I lived in poverty and encountered racism throughout my entire childhood. I was inspired to write this book about my childhood because my granddaughter is asking questions about race. We owe it to her and other children to honestly answer her questions. I was a curious child and had my own set of questions about the way we were living. My parents explained some people feel differently about other people. Sometimes, they may not know why they feel that way. As children, they may have seen the way their parents behaved.

The way they felt and thought was not discussed and became twisted together and confused like a tangled web. When they got older, things got worse. The tangled web got bigger and no one tried to untangle it.

It is time to join together and untangle the web. We owe it to our current and future generations!

Where's Tippy?

Francie Mae, come in the house right now! The little curly haired girl was pedaling a faded red bicycle with one missing pedal around the old house where they lived. The house was so run down it was now called a shack. The peeling paint on the shack told a story that it was once white and stately. The bicycle's frame had a glimmer of red but was now rusted. Francie Mae didn't care about the shack or bicycle. She was trying to figure out how to make the bicycle go faster without two pedals. She was slightly irritated that her mother called her inside before she could figure it out.

When she got to the big fig tree that was in the front yard, she hopped off the worn bicycle to see what her mother wanted. Her once braided long curly black hair fell into an unruly mop of half braided curls. I declare, "I don't know what I am going to do with your hair", said her mother. She shook her head and guided her youngest child into the house. Francie Mae loved playing outdoors but also knew her home was a place of comfort. When she entered the worn doors of the shack, she was in a loving home filled with family, laughter and hope. She was surprised that her older siblings, Lil Bro, Vie and Rom were already in the house. Like her, they enjoyed playing outside. "Stay in the house until I tell you to come out" their mother said in a firm voice. By the tone of her voice, they knew she meant what she said. Without another word, she grabbed her apron, and went into the kitchen to start dinner. Francie Mae and her siblings looked at each other but didn't dare say a word. They wondered why they were told to stay in the house while their oldest brother, Tippy, was not in the house. Their father was not in the house either.

Francie Mae was a curious girl and wanted to know what was going on. She had a plan. She peeked in the direction of the kitchen to make sure their mother was still there. She tiptoed across the plank wood floor toward the window, being careful not to step on the rotten board that always made a creaking sound. When she was sure she was safe, she bravely moved the newspaper that was covering the broken window in the front room and peeked out.

She saw her father standing by the road, near the mailbox. Standing with him was Tippy, her older cousin Fessor and some men she didn't know. They were out of earshot of anyone in the shack and seemed to talk excitedly with their hands. From inside the cramped front room, she heard the voice of her sister warning her to get away from the window. Ignoring her advice, she continued to stare. It felt like she was in a trance. After what seemed like forever, she saw the group of men and Tippy walk hurriedly toward the house. The next morning, Tippy was gone.

Becoming Francie Mae

Francie Mae was born and grew up in poverty in the south. She was the youngest of five children. She and her family lived on farm land that was owned by the local white constable. He was known to be a mean man and owned most of the land in the town they lived in. The rich soil on the land was perfect for cotton production and it became the major crop in the south. In order to grow enough cotton to make a crop, a large number of workers were needed. These workers were mostly poor black people. To make money to buy basic needs, Francie Mae's parents and her older siblings' chopped cotton all day in the hot summers and picked cotton all day in the fall. These jobs did not pay much money and they never had enough food to eat. Her parents struggled to save money because there were no jobs between crop production times.

Things were different during those times. There were laws that made things unequal for people of different races. At fifteen years old, Tippy was ten years older than Francie Mae. He and their brother, Lil Bro, were a year apart and acted like twins. Lil Bro was the tallest but Tippy never forgot to tell him he wasn't the oldest. Tippy was very smart and talkative. Lil Bro was very smart but more thoughtful. Both were talented artists and musicians. Francie Mae loved it when Lil Bro babysat them. He never tired of answering her many questions. Their sister Vie was the middle child and with her high cheekbones, had a striking appearance. She had a gift for making everything she touched look pretty. Francie Mae adored her big sister and wanted to be like her. The youngest brother Rom, had light brown eyes like their father, and also had a mop of curly black hair. He was three years older than Francie Mae and spoke in a firm voice like their mother.

Unlike her siblings, Francie Mae had a round face and big brown eyes. Secretly, she wished she had high cheek bones like her sister Vie, light brown eyes like her brother Rom, and the talents of Tippy and Lil Bro. She was a curious child with a thirst for knowledge. She figured she was smart enough because she liked to figure things out. She enjoyed reading, lively dancing, running in the grass with her bare feet, and laughing out loud. Even though she lived in poverty, she was happy. She had a mother, father, and siblings and that was enough for her. Plus, she had a vivid imagination that kept her busy.

There were no toys or children nearby to play with so her imagination became her daily companion. When she got tired of riding her rusty bicycle, making mud pies and drawing stick fingers in the clay dirt, she kept herself busy by pestering her older siblings. She thought her long curly hair was a nuisance because it never stayed in place. She went to school with her hair neatly braided but by the end of the day, her braids were unraveled and a mop of unruly curls took their place.

On school days, she walked to the bus stop with Rom to ride the big yellow school bus that would take them on a long ride to and from elementary school. Vie and Lil Bro rode a long way on another big yellow school bus to go to another school. As a young child, she sensed something was not right. There had to be a good reason that Tippy was no longer living at home. She missed her big brother and was determined to find out the reason he left.

Shortly after Tippy left, they moved and lived in another shack surrounded by cotton fields. This shack was in worse shape than the first one. It was hard to imagine how it once looked because there was not a hint of color. It stood un-sturdy on what seemed like wobbly legs. The worn tin roof tried it's best to protect the three rooms there were lined up behind each other from the front to the back. The front and back doors had broken latches that their father had to fix. The front porch had seen much better days. It creaked every time someone stepped on the rotted wood. Francie Mae learned how to step in the right places so she didn't fall to the murky dirt below. She didn't care about living in the shack. She wanted to know where her big brother was. Things were different without Tippy.

Francie Mae knew she had a choice to make. The only way she would know the answer to her question was to ask her parents. If her older siblings knew, they didn't tell her. They probably thought she was too young to understand. It had been a year since Tippy left. She was six years old and her curiosity got the best of her. She had to know what happened to Tippy.

Discovering the Truth

Image credit to Clifford Hewlett
Title-In the Autumn of Life

Francie Mae finally got the courage to ask her parents the reason for Tippy's sudden departure. Her father looked at her with sadness in his light brown eyes. Normally his eyes twinkled and he always wore a smile. She studied her mother's face but it was hard to know what she was thinking. Her mother absently brushed her unruly curly hair back from her eyes with her hand. They both looked in her frightened big wide eyes.

"I hope you understand what we are going to tell you", said her father. Francie Mae nodded her head yes but was scared inside. Satisfied with her answer he continued. "Tippy had to leave and live with Cousin Fessor so he could finish school. He couldn't finish school where we lived before. A grown man threatened to hurt him if he didn't drop out and work in the cotton field. He is a smart boy and stood up for himself. They had to leave in the middle of the night so no one would see them. We had to move for the same reason. Things are not fair for black people and it is not right. It has been that way for a long time and will take a long time for it to change. Do you understand?"

Francie Mae sadly nodded her head yes. At six years old, she was old enough to see differences in color and how people are treated. She thought about when she went to the grocery store with her father and heard white men call black men "boy" and black women "gal". She saw black men look down at their feet when white men talked with them. They were all adult men. She thought it was strange that they didn't look in each other's eyes. She never saw her father look down or answer to "boy." She was angry and wanted to know who this grown man was that threatened to hurt her big brother. He didn't commit a crime; he wanted to go to school.

As they walked, she noticed the big pretty houses white people lived in and the shacks poor black people lived in. She heard the ugly words white people yelled out the window of their cars and trucks when they passed by them. She saw the flags that were waved angrily in their direction. The flags didn't look like the American flags she had in her classroom. Sometimes, they had to jump into the overgrown bushes when they heard the sounds of the vehicles approaching so they wouldn't be seen. The curls fell down in her face again but this time she didn't care. She buried herself in the arms of her mother and father as the tears fell from her little round face. She felt the sting of racism and it didn't feel right.

Francie Mae loved walking to the grocery store with her father. She thought he was brave and he protected them. He was a friendly, talkative man and got along with everyone. When they got to the store, the friendly grocery store owner looked over his wire framed glasses and greeted them with a smile. He was white but not mean. He let her father buy groceries and pay him later. He gave her father cookies or candy to take home to her siblings and gave her a lollipop. He always said "Every child needs a little lick of flavor." She didn't understand why everyone wasn't kind like the friendly grocery store owner.

When she got older, Lil Bro told her more about Tippy's sudden departure. The town constable was the man that threatened Tippy for standing up for his right to go to school. This was a man that was supposed to protect people, not threaten them. Francie Mae and her family lived on the constable's land and worked in his cotton fields. He and many other white people thought black people were only supposed to work in the cotton fields and not go to school. Those thoughts didn't make sense to her. The friendly white grocery store owner didn't feel that way. She wondered why more people didn't feel like him.

It was necessary for her to know the truth. She knew that some people were unkind and some were kind. She was curious to know why so many seemed unkind. She wondered why some people were poor and some were wealthy. She was curious to know how poor people could be wealthy. She wondered why people with darker skin colors were treated differently from people with lighter skin colors. She was curious to know why people of all races were not treated the same. She was curious to know why some people remained silent when people were mistreated. In the meantime, she had to cling onto hope that things would change for the better.

She missed Tippy but was happy that he stood up for what was right. She knew this was not easy for him to do. Tippy lived with Cousin Fessor until he graduated from high school. He came home during the summer and on some weekends. She was always happy to see him. Over the years they spent time catching up. He looked happy and was thriving. He was taking piano lessons from a real piano teacher. He was playing the trumpet in the school band. He received recognition for his public speaking abilities by winning a city wide oratorical contest. He was elected president of his senior class and the student council. In these leadership roles, he was able to represent the senior class and the entire student body. He earned a scholarship to go to college. After graduating from high school, he moved to another state and enrolled in a private college. This felt right. She knew Tippy would do well so she vowed to stop missing him so much.

Francie Mae learned the value of getting an education. It was a key to unlocking the many questions she had. It was her key to get out of poverty and stay out of poverty. She knew it would not be easy but she had to do it! She and her siblings rode long distances to and from school but found that learning was exciting. If she wanted to escape from poverty, she had to go to school and learn.

As she got older, she became aware that many things were not fair for black people. Her mother explained it to her in a way she could understand. "Francie Mae, your hair is long and curly. If we don't comb and brush your hair every day, it will be tangled. It's easy for hair to tangle but hard to get it untangled. It hurts but you have to keep combing and brushing. Soon the tangles disappear. You never want your hair to be tangled again. It's like a web; it's easy to get caught in it but hard to get out." Francie Mae knew how tangled hair felt and cringed at the thought.

Francie Mae knew this was true because she entertained herself on many days watching spiders spin a web to trap flies. Some never made it out. They did not have help. She watched her mother sew patches on their used clothes. Sometimes all she had to use was old yarn. She used whatever colors she could find to make the patches. She helped her mother untangle the yarn so it could be used. They had to work together. When she finished, there were many different and beautiful colors on one piece of cloth.

She learned that people were caught in a tangled web from years ago and no one tried to untangle it. Some people were fearful and some were indifferent. Some people added more tangles to the web. With education, she learned many people were willing to help make things fair. It takes a lot of people to untangle the web but if everyone pulls a string, it will eventually unravel. She clung to hope that with everyone working together, the web would untangle and become something beautiful.

Laws of the South

Francie Mae and her family lived in the south. Laws were different then. There were state and local laws called Jim Crow laws. These laws were based on race. They enforced separation of black and white people in public places such as schools, transportation, restrooms and restaurants. There were separate drinking fountains, waiting rooms at the doctor's offices and separate hospitals. These laws also made it hard for black people to get stable housing, a good job and to vote. These laws told black people where to live, work, play and who to marry.

Francie Mae saw this happening almost every day. She didn't like what she was seeing. These laws kept black and white people from having the same opportunities. Some of these laws spread to other states. When she went downtown with her family, she saw big signs posted marked "colored" and "white". These signs were used to show people of color where they were not allowed to go or do. There were separate rules for black and white people living in the same country.

These laws were called unjust because they discriminated against people of color. These laws made her feel bad. She remembered what her mother told her about the tangled web and thought, "If a web is tangled, why not try to untangle it. That would be the right thing to do." Francie Mae was puzzled why people allowed these mean laws. She met some people who were kind and wondered why they didn't help untangle the web.

Francie Mae's father served in the Army but was not able to get a job after serving his country. This was part of the tangled web. As a result, she and her family lived in shacks without electricity or indoor plumbing. Without income, they had no money to buy basic necessities like food and clothes. Local farmers grew cotton and it was plentiful. They lived in the big pretty houses and drove new shiny cars. Their children had toys and went to neighborhood schools. To earn money, Francie Mae and her family spent long hours in the cotton field chopping and picking the cotton the farmers planted.

She was too young to understand these unequal laws but knew they were not right. She questioned why people had different laws because of their skin color. She began a journey to discover the answers to her many questions. She learned to observe, listen, and ask more questions. When she got older, she knew she had to find out about her ancestors. Even though it was a long time ago, she knew she had to know their story. There must be a reason why they were trapped in a tangled web and no one helped pull the strings. Their story will help reveal the truth.

When she got older, Francie Mae loved to learn and read books. She asked her parents questions if she didn't find the answers in the books. Lil Bro also loved to read and he knew a lot about their ancestors. He was happy to tell her the story and answer her many questions. She learned that her ancestors were slaves. A long time ago, they were kidnapped from their African homelands, put in chains and brought to America to work in crop fields like cotton. Most of the slaves were in the southern states. The southern states wanted to keep slaves to work in the cotton fields. There was a war between citizens in the same country. This war was called a civil war and was fought between the northern and southern states to determine if slavery was legal or the right thing to do. The slaves in Texas were not free until June 19, 1865. When they learned of their freedom, celebrations called Juneteenth occurred.

The president during that time was Abraham Lincoln; he developed a plan to win the south by issuing the Emancipation Proclamation on January 1, 1863. This important document freed the slaves in the southern states that were fighting to keep slaves. In 1865, the 13th Amendment to the

Constitution made slavery illegal in all states because it was not the right thing to do. The Constitution is the supreme law and has more power than state and local laws. After abolishing slavery, a decision was made to keep white people and black people separate. The Supreme Court supported the idea. The Supreme Court is the highest court in the United States. In a court case, the court said separate but equal was fair.

As Francie Mae read, she knew this was not fair or right. She also knew that many other people felt the same way as she did. This was part of the tangled web that no one wanted to untangle. She was now twelve years old and was feeling the effects of laws based on the color of her skin. She learned the name of the flag that was waved angrily by some of the local white people. She had lived in poverty all her life and was tired of living that way. She and her family were living in another shack on another rich farmers land and working in his cotton fields for low wages. After a while, all the shacks and farmland looked the same. Seven years had passed since Tippy left and things were not better for black people.

Francie Mae was still searching for the answers to her questions and hoped to find some answers in the many books she read. She grabbed one of her father's worn paperback books and scurried outside to read under her favorite oak tree on the side of the shack.

Many years ago when our country was formed, a set of beliefs and values were attributed to a group of people. These beliefs are called ideologies. Many of these ideologies were based on assumptions and not facts. These ideologies were racist and were passed from generation to generation and never questioned. This was not right.

She took a break from reading and saw an eagle soaring in the sky like he didn't have a care in the world. He used his long broad wings to lift himself higher. She imagined what it would feel like to sit on the wings of the eagle and look down and see the world from a different view. She wondered what it felt like to fly and feel the breeze against her face. When she got tired, all she had to do was lift herself up like that powerful eagle. "That's it!" shouted Francie Mae to anyone within hearing distance. "I'm going to be strong and powerful like an eagle. If I'm strong and powerful, I can help untangle the web."

Even though there were schools in her neighborhood, she and her siblings rode on a school bus for thirty two miles round trip to go to school.

All the students, teachers and workers were black. She met other students and teachers who felt the same way she did. They wanted to help untangle the web. In the meantime, they were devoted to providing the students with a good education. They made learning fun!

Francie Mae was strong like the eagle and decided to learn everything she could. She learned that education was power. She and her family lived in the last shack at the bottom of a long dirt road. Every school day, she waited patiently by the run down mailbox for the big yellow school bus to appear. The kind and fatherly bus driver was one of the men in the community. His children went to the same school. She dreaded the long ride but school also gave her the opportunity to be inside a big brick building, and talk and play with other children her age. There were no big signs marked "colored" and "white." She breathed a sigh of relief.

In their classrooms, they pledged allegiance to the flag each morning. They had no understanding of what the pledge meant. During assemblies, they sang the National Anthem. They didn't understand the words of the song either. They grew up pledging allegiance to a U.S. flag that promised liberty and justice for all, yet they lived and felt the sting of exclusion based on their skin color. They sang a song about freedom but didn't feel free. They did as they were told.

She was determined to go to school and get an education. Having an education seemed to be the best path out of poverty. She went to school hungry on many days. There was never enough food to eat. Hunger pangs became her constant companion. Many days, her parents did without so their children could eat. She knew her teachers would make sure she and other poor children had lunch to eat. No person should be hungry because of unfair laws. She had to help untangle the web so she and her family could get out of poverty.

The Fig Tree

On the weekends and after her chores were done, Francie Mae had more time to read. On nice days, she busied herself by reading outside. The beautiful sky seemed to watch from overhead. Reading books provided knowledge and a temporary escape from a life of poverty. The beautiful trees and open farmland became her playground.

She and her family worked in the cotton fields during the week. In the summer, they chopped cotton and picked cotton in the fall. Between cotton seasons, every day except Sunday, her father put on worn overalls and work boots and left home early. He was working odd jobs to feed his hungry family. Her mother always wore an apron over her long tattered dress. When she was happy, she hummed to herself. This day, she hummed as she kept herself busy with other chores. She seemed to never run out of things to do.

Her older siblings had their own interests. Vie kept herself busy decorating the shack with colorful flowers or helping their mother cook. Lil Bro was a budding artist and was busy sketching anything he saw.

When he tired of sketching, he practiced blowing the saxophone that he got from school. Rom was the quietest and loved to tinker with old radios and bicycles. When the repairs were done, a wide smile appeared across his usually stern looking face. In their own way, they were trying to add beauty and make sense of a world that seemed to forget them.

Francie Mae read one of her father's books, *Native Son* by Richard Wright. The book explained the racial divide in America by social conditions imposed on black people by white people. She kept reading in an effort to understand the actions of the main character named Bigger Thomas.

As she read, the spring breeze blew softly across her face, turning the pages of the book before she was ready. She shifted her body slightly to block some of the breeze. This was the first book she read by a black author and she wanted to read every word that was written. The story was about a poor black family living in Chicago. This city was a long way from where she lived but was where her father grew up. Since the family lived in Chicago, they didn't live under the same Jim Crow laws but had similar struggles based on their race. They lived in a ghetto in a big city and some of the struggles included crime. According to the author, in a strange way, this made them feel alive and provided comfort. Like the characters in the book she was reading, she realized that some people in poverty seemed to cling to any form of comfort. Some may be good and some may be bad.

Wright wrote "Black people are the necessary product of the society that formed them and told them since birth exactly who they were supposed to be." The main character was conscious of a system of racial oppression that leaves him no opportunity to exist but through crimes. In a world attracted to wealth, crime is a reaction to the environment. The author wrote that Bigger drank alcohol to forget his hard life. His life of crime was the only thing he owned. Wright wrote "Everyone has a hunger for life that must be fulfilled." Unfortunately, sometimes this hunger involves a life of crime. In the character, Bigger's case, crime was the most meaningful thing that ever happened to him. This didn't feel right but it was a painful reality.

Francie Mae took a break from reading and thought about the earlier days. As long as she could remember cotton fields were as far as her eyes could see. She thought that there had to be more to life than poverty, crime and cotton fields. Her first memory was of the shack she and her family lived in when Tippy left. The old fig tree in the front yard was her comfort. It always produced ripe juicy figs once or twice a year. Sometimes, her mother picked the figs from the tree and made preserves. She and her family always had delicious fruit to eat. She loved to ride her old bicycle around the house in circles. When she got tired, she stopped and rested under the protective shade of the big fig tree. She had to find meaning in her life that didn't involve crime.

She and her family walked about a mile to and from church on Sundays. Once inside the small red brick building with a white steeple on top, she hurried to the small classroom to join her friends. She learned about the parable of the barren fig tree in Sunday school. Fig trees produce good figs or bad figs. The bad figs couldn't be eaten. If you take care of the fig tree, it will produce good figs that can be enjoyed. You have to throw the rotten figs away. She remembered that many figs fell from the tree to the ground. As hungry as they were, her mother never picked up those figs to make preserves. She compared the character in the book she was reading to all things, figs! The character grew up in church. He became restless and began a life of crime. He was looking for comfort. Instead of choosing the good fig, he chose the path of the bad fig that dropped to the ground. He didn't feel like he had another choice.

Francie Mae learned that like the good fig, God will watch over and protect His people. This was the beginning of her faith. They may not have much, laws may not be the same, but she knew that someday, things would get better. As she got older, she figured she may look for comfort and didn't want to make the wrong choices. There may be some bad figs in life but she knew she had to be like the good fig. She had to always remember to take care of herself and treat everyone the same.

Francie Mae had lived in poverty her entire childhood but she had a happy home. She remembered the first shack they moved in after Tippy left. It sat in the middle of a huge cotton field. The winters in the shotgun shack at that location were treacherous. The wind howled like a hungry wolf. Ice hung from the tin roof like glaciers. She and her siblings knocked the ice hanging from the tin roof of the shack and pretended they had popsicles. The cold wind seeped in through the cracks in the wall and floor.

It felt like they were living outside. Her mother paste old newspapers on the walls and put raggedly quilts up to the windows in an effort to keep out the draft. This was no match for the strong winds. The wood burning stove tried it's best to keep them warm but it was not enough for the icy and cold winter nights. One night, her feet were frost bitten while sleeping.

They never had enough food to eat. When she was in first grade, she fainted on the school grounds due to hunger. When she woke up, the teachers and students were gathered around her. She saw the fright in their wide eyes. She learned that the teachers at school were caring. There was a national school lunch program but she and her family didn't know about it. The teachers gave her and other poor students food to eat. She learned about food called commodities that was provided to poor families by the United States government.

She remembered when Lil Bro got sick. Their parents knew he needed to see a doctor. There was no medical insurance for poor people. They didn't have a car, money or a telephone so her father walked to find someone to take him to the charity hospital. She walked with him and saw the fear in this brave man's eyes. Since they lived on a farm, they had to walk a long way. White families lived near the farm. He knocked on many doors and no one was willing to help. After going from house to house, they were tired. At the last house, a kind looking white man opened the door. Her father explained the reason for the visit. He tried to close the door but Francie Mae spoke up. In a voice that was beyond her six years she asked the man, "What if this was your child that needed help?" He grabbed his hat and this kind hearted man took them back to their shack before taking her father and Lil Bro to the hospital. Lil Bro had emergency surgery due to a ruptured appendix. She couldn't imagine the fear her parents had thinking their child would die because they couldn't help him.

Francie Mae could not get this vision out of her head. She didn't understand why people were not willing to help each other. She continued to learn every day. When school was out, she read as much as she could. She lived in a shack but there was beauty around her. She stretched her bare feet out and felt the green blades of the grass tickle her toes. Nearby, an orange butterfly landed on the delicate garden of wild flowers. She watched as it chose a flower to rest on and spread its colorful wings. When it tired of the flower, it moved to the next one.

By this time, her eyes were heavy from reading and her brain was tired from remembering. The cool breeze had found its way to where she shifted her body. The small paperback book felt like it weighed a ton. She gently let go of her grip as if she was releasing the weight of the world. Before she drifted off to sleep, she made a promise to be like the fig tree in the front yard and produce good fruit.

The Dream is Not a Dream

As she continued to nap under the protective leaves of the big oak tree, she learned answers to some of her questions. The thick trunk of the tree provided the perfect pillow. The hard bark provided comfort in a time that was not comforting. She had to know the truth so she could help untangle the web. She realized that many people didn't help because of fear. Many people wanted to help but the laws were different. The brave man who took her father and Lil Bro to the hospital and the kind grocer helped pull strings to help untangle the web.

Francie Mae's family and other black families felt the effects of slavery for many years. The slave system grew out of plantation life. The constitution eventually made slavery illegal but southern laws called Jim Crow laws prevented black people from having equal opportunities. The southern states were rich and grew crops of cotton, tobacco and rice. Some southern people thought slaves and black people were supposed to work in the fields for free or for little money. Sadly, many other people thought the same way. They elected people to political office who shared the same beliefs. These people appointed people to positions that felt the same way. Many police and law enforcement officers felt the same way. They added to the tangled web.

She learned that many black families left the south to look for jobs and other opportunities in other states. This was called The Great Migration. Her father's family moved to the north when he was a child and settled in Chicago. She learned that he was the youngest of 10 male children born to a black father whose parents were slaves. His parents passed away before she was born. His mother was white and Native American. She was called biracial because she was a combination of two races. During those times, people of different races could not marry or live together in the south. Francie Mae realized her father's eyes were light brown like his mother and her unruly black hair was curly and long like her grandmother. Francie Mae and her siblings called their father, Dad.

Her father went back to the south as a grown-up and met her mother. Her mother was a strong-willed woman who was raised on a farm and lived all her life in the south. She was the oldest of 10 children and born to parents whose parents were slaves. Her mother's skin dark skin was so beautiful it looked like it was kissed by the sun. Her parents passed away when Francie Mae was young. Now, she knew why her brothers and sisters had different beautiful shades of skin colors and hair textures. If they could live together and love each other with different skin colors, she didn't understand why other people couldn't. Francie Mae and her siblings called their mother, MaDear. Many black families called their mothers, Madea, Muhdea, or other variations. These names are traditional combinations of Mother Dear.

When Francie Mae was growing up, black people were called different names. Some of the names didn't feel right. Eventually, black people whose ancestors came from Africa were called African-Americans. Some black people's ancestors came from other areas. Francie Mae's ancestors came from Africa and she was also an African-American. She didn't know where her paternal grandmother came from. She was proud of her beautiful, strong, and courageous ancestors. She was now proud of her unruly mop of curly hair and the beautiful shades of skin God gave her family. She knew why she liked to dance lively to the beat of music that sometimes was only in her head. She knew why she liked to laugh out loud. She was honored to be a living picture of her ancestors.

When Francie Mae was eleven years old, she volunteered to work in the library at school and checked out books to take home. She wanted to know why the web was still tangled. She thought the answers were in books. Some of her favorite books were *To Kill a Mockingbird* by Harper Lee and *Little Women* by Louisa May Alcott. She was intrigued by the power and strength of the characters. In the book, *To Kill a Mockingbird*, she was saddened by the racial injustice. She was rooting for a happy ending for the falsely accused black man but it didn't happen. She was proud of the brave white lawyer who represented him. Even in a book, there was no happy ending. Mockingbirds represent innocence and an innocent man was convicted by an all-white jury of a crime he didn't commit. More false beliefs were added to the web and it did not untangle.

When she read, she tried to ignore the nearby cotton fields. She learned that it was not until the 1954 case of Brown vs Board of Education that the Supreme Court ruled that separate is not equal. Schools in the south were ordered to accept all students but this didn't happen right away. Black people demanded equal rights that were given to them by the Constitution and later the Supreme Court. When this didn't happen, the Civil Rights Movement started. The civil rights workers tried to untangle the web. She couldn't believe what she was reading what she was now living.

Even though black people lived in the same country as white people, they were treated differently. An organization was formed by black leaders to fight for justice and equal rights. A minister named Dr. Martin Luther King was one of many black and white leaders in the fight for civil rights. Because of these laws, black people had to live and play by a long list of separate rules. They had to sit at the back of the bus, go to separate schools, use separate water fountains, use separate restrooms, use separate waiting rooms at the doctor's offices, and could not vote.

Black people and white people who wanted to help fight against these rules and laws began fighting for justice. They were trained to be peaceful and learned how to stay calm. Many people were arrested, jailed, beaten, and killed. In 1963, Dr. King gave a powerful speech in Washington, D.C. called "I Have a Dream". About two hundred and fifty thousand people attended the rally. This speech was a message of hope. White people and

Black people joined together and supported the same cause. This rally helped to bring about the Civil Rights Act of 1964. This act promised equal rights to all people regardless of race, religion, gender or national origin.

Francie Mae was encouraged and excited by what she learned. There were people willing to untangle the web and fix what was wrong. It didn't seem that Cousin Fessor was caught in the web. He lived in a brick home in the city, owned a business and was not living in poverty. Plus, he took Tippy in. He had to know the secret of getting out of poverty. "I know" she exclaimed in her dream, "I will ask him the next time I see him!"

A Camp Divided

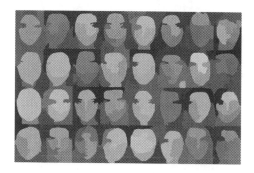

Francie Mae didn't expect to experience prejudice within her own race. Her best friend BB invited her to go with her to summer camp for vacation Bible school. The camp was for girls in junior high school or entering junior high. She was eleven years old and was looking forward to starting junior high in the fall and meeting new friends. She previously attended vacation Bible school during the summer at the local church and knew most of the girls. They met at the small local red brick church. The group of girls and their chaperones loaded on the school bus. The girls couldn't contain their excitement. Many had never been to camp. They laughed and giggled with excitement all the way to their campsite.

She begged her mother to let her go to summer camp but didn't expect to be bullied. She certainly didn't expect this behavior at a church related activity. When they got to the camp site, there were girls from other towns that they didn't know. They were all black and from different socio-economic backgrounds. The church sponsored chaperones and camp counselors assigned cabins based on age. Eleven and twelve year olds shared cabins and thirteen years and older shared cabins. Francie Mae was almost twelve and in a cabin separate from BB, who was a year older. They saw each other during classes and at meal time. The first day went off without a hitch. Since she loved being outdoors, she was adjusting to camping and making new friends from other communities and schools.

She noted that some of the girls gathered in their own clique. They were well dressed and wore their hair in curls or straight. They wore colorful headbands or pretty barrettes as hair ornaments. She was particularly interested in their hair because her own hair was so curly and unruly. She wanted to know how they convinced their parents to let them style their hair at their age. BB and her other classmates didn't wear their hair in curls or straight. Vie and her friends straightened their hair and wore it in curls or other styles but they were in high school. She looked forward to talking with this group of girls to learn how to manage her hair. BB, a few other girls and Francie Mae decided to talk with them. They totally ignored them and continued talking among themselves. They immediately knew they were not welcome in this group.

She tried to forget about the girls but couldn't help but notice them. They were assigned various activities to keep busy. They had outdoor living skills classes, Bible study classes, arts and crafts, dance and swimming classes. After a hot breakfast, they were given lunch in a brown paper bag. They sat outside on picnic benches and enjoyed their lunch. BB and Francie Mae attended the same dance classes. This was an opportunity to perfect the moves they learned earlier. She learned how to do a dance called "The Mashed Potatoes" and with BB's input, learned some fancier dance moves. The clique girls attended the same classes but stuck together and continued to ignore them like they didn't exist.

Around mid- week, Francie Mae was looking for BB and entered a cabin for the thirteen and over girls and went to the wrong room. There were three bigger girls in the room. They appeared older than the rest of the girls. The biggest girl glared from her top bunk at Francie Mae and asked why she was in their room. The two other girls were sitting in chairs near the bottom bunk and glaring at her. As bravely as she could, she told them she was looking for BB. The girl on the top bunk glanced at the other girls, smiled and then glared back at Francie Mae. She knew she had walked in a danger zone.

From her perch on top of the bed, the girl hurled verbal insults and the other two girls laughed their approval. Francie Mae was surprised and hurt at the same time. She had seen Francie Mae dancing in class and decided to tease her. "I want you to do The Mashed Potatoes" she said. Francie Mae thought she wouldn't tease her anymore after she saw how well she danced, so she did as she demanded. The girl smiled but was not through with her yet. She said, "Girl, you must think you're something because you can dance and you have good hair". Other than being a curly nuisance, she never gave that much thought to her hair. She was standing near the door but didn't think to dash out of it. Even with a safe exit, she felt paralyzed by fear and was trapped by the girls' words. She continued to berate Francie Mae and the other two girls joined in. They called her a poor girl and made fun of her clothes. They wanted to know why she was at camp. By this time, they were glaring at her like she was a piece of trash. Their words hurt. She thought, "Where were her parents to shield her from this danger?"

She didn't realize it but she was being bullied. The girl on the top bunk was the apparent ring leader and the other girls laughed and did what she said. Glaring girl was not finished with Francie Mae yet. They were darker and decided to talk about her skin tone. She ordered one of the girls to give her one of the brown paper bags that their lunches were in. She jumped down from her perch and placed the brown paper bag next to Francie Mae's skin. "See you got that long curly hair but you are not light skinned. Plus, you are poor!" The two other girls laughed harder.

The negative comments continued. Francie Mae had to get out of that room. At the time, she didn't realize she didn't have to do anything they said. Nothing was holding her there but her own fear. She felt the tears well up in my eyes but was determined not to cry. She was humiliated and she didn't like it one bit. As the girl's tirades continued and the laughter got louder, her fear turned to rage. Instead of going out the open door, she looked around the room to see what weapon she could use to defend herself in case it was needed. She wanted to hurt them like they hurt her. This time, she was surprised by her own emotions. She had never felt rage before and it scared her.

Something strange happened as she was pondering her next move. She imagined that she heard the voice of her parents. When they were yelled at and called derogatory names by racists, they instructed them not to react.

"Keep your head up Francie Mae" she heard them say in her imagination. She remembered the many conversations she had with her family. She was taught that the civil right workers were trained in non-violent protests. When they were beaten, they didn't react. She couldn't cower. She had to use her voice and speak with confidence as her father taught her. There is a saying, "sticks and stones may break my bones but words will never hurt me." These words hurt! Since these bullies didn't move towards her, she figured they were all talk. Her parents taught her that people can say whatever they want; just don't let it be true.

Using a voice that was powerful beyond her years, she told them she was not going to do what they asked any longer. With that, she turned around and walked out of the open door and didn't look back. She didn't tell the church chaperones, counselors or her parents about the bullying. She told BB and identified the girls just in case they tried to bully her again but they didn't. As a precaution, she found the perfect rock and kept it in her pocket for protection.

She went to vacation Bible school to have fun and learn stories from the Bible. She didn't know that interacting with a group of people would cause conflict and division. She learned Bible stories and life stories as well. They were a group of children in various developmental stages and were learning about life and themselves. Most of them had never been away from home. They were learning how to develop competence in their own interpersonal and social relationships. They were learning their own identities and trying new ways of thinking and behaving.

After the bullying episode, Francie Mae didn't like the humiliation, fear or rage. When she was bullied, she did not exchange words with the bully. She didn't know it at the time but exchanging words could have led to heated exchanges or a fight. It is a natural response to try to react to hurtful words. To think with a clear head, she had to control her own fear and anger. She didn't like being bullied and vowed to never bully anyone.

Later in life, she realized that most bullies are cowards and they use their perceived power to play mind games. She had control of her behavior but didn't realize it. Words could only hurt her if she allowed it. She learned that as long as we interact with people, there will be conflicts and a need for effective conflict resolution. This was another string of the web to untangle.

Classism and Colorism

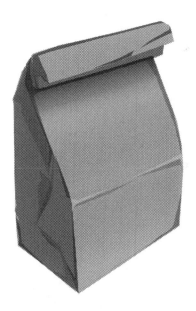

In addition to being bullied, Francie Mae experienced classism and colorism in her own race. Classism and colorism can be complicated and confusing. Some black people adopted society's biases in an effort to fit in. Historically, black people were marginalized based on slavery and Jim Crow laws and tried to create an internal culture that mirrored whites.

Classism may be defined as prejudice against or in favor of people belonging to a particular social class. These people may think they are superior to poor or disadvantaged people. In black culture, these people may be considered elite or snobs. During the time Francie Mae was growing up, they were a group of people who shared similar economic and social positions based on income. The girls she encountered during vacation Bible school were most likely the children of more affluent parents. They acted in the manner they were accustomed to. Sometimes people who are poor keep their feelings inside and feel inferior to higher income people. Internalizing feelings is not a healthy outlet and can cause stress.

Colorism is a historical injustice that gave lighter skinned black people access to a better life. Some black people used a brown paper bag to compare skin tones. Historically, the thought was that lighter skinned people had access to a better life and darker skinned people were thought to have fewer privileges. Historically, biological differences in skin tones were used for justification of oppression. Slaves with lighter skin worked in their master's houses and darker skinned slaves worked hard labor in the fields. These unfounded ideologies prevented many people from seeking out better opportunities in life.

Francie Mae was curious and used a brown paper bag to measure her skin tone. She and her siblings had a combination of many skin tones and physical features. This was also true for her mother and father. She realized that it didn't matter how their skins compared to the paper bag. It didn't matter about the appearance of their physical features. What mattered is they were all one loving family.

Many people are a combination of other races. They have mixed heritage and may be called bi-racial or multi-racial. Society has pressured people to choose one race based on the one drop rule. If a person has a black parent, they are considered black. Sometimes their own family members may make hurtful comments about race. Sometimes the lighter skinned siblings may be treated more favorably. Darker skinned children may feel devalued and may not know how to communicate how they feel.

Many mixed race children feel scorn and rejection from their peers. Francie Mae went to school with children whose skin tones were lighter than hers. She went to school with children whose eye colors were different from hers. Sometimes these children were called names that didn't sound right. She went to school with children whose hair was longer or straighter than hers. Their physical appearance didn't matter. What mattered to her was if they were friendly and kind. They were her classmates and friends.

There was a lot of emphasis placed on hair as a characteristic of beauty and acceptance. Many black people used "bleaching skin creams" in an effort to lighten their skin. European looking hair was considered "good hair." Many girls straightened their hair to achieve this look. Francie Mae's hair was long and curly. The thought was that straight or long curly hair was good and coarser hair was perceived as "bad" hair. These unjust measuring devices created division between black people. A person's hair, skin color, or economic status does not define who they are. This was another way colonization programmed some black people to believe the way they looked was inferior. This didn't feel right.

Classism and colorism can be complicated and confusing. Some black people adopted society's biases in an effort to fit in. People should be accepted and valued for who they are. People with higher economic status do not possess all the power and success. Everyone makes a contribution. The bullies have no power at all. Bullies may be children or adults who seek to harm people they perceive as vulnerable. It is hard to know why people bully. Some are rewarded for their behaviors. Others are hiding behind their own insecurities.

Francie Mae was never bullied again but racism, discrimination, classism and colorism continued on the journey with her. Sexism decided to hitch a ride also. On her journey to adulthood, she had to learn to face and confront these giants without fear. She couldn't allow someone else biases to make her believe she was a victim of other people's decisions and choices. They have to help pull strings to untangle the web.

Conversations around the Pot Belly Stove

By now, Francie Mae had napped for about thirty minutes. She was not ready to wake up from a dream of information. The cool breeze continued to blow gently across her face. Absently, she reached her hand out as if trying to find a sweater. After realizing she didn't have one, she shifted positions and before she knew it, she was lulled back to sleep.

Francie Mae and her family had a cast-iron black stove with a pot belly that was located in the center room of their shack. In the late fall and early winter, they sat around the stove to talk about what was happening in the United States. They had a break from the laborious tasks of chopping and picking cotton. This was their time to gather around the old stove and talk. As they talked, they couldn't help but stare at the flames. The stove provided some warmth and comfort in a world that seemed cold. The bulge in the middle of the stove seemed to swell as if it could absorb their in-depth conversations. It didn't make sense that people were hurt while fighting for equal justice. All people couldn't enjoy the same rights.

When Cousin Fessor and Tippy came to visit, they joined them around the stove they named Pot Belly. Cousin Fessor was an educated man. He was an attorney and teacher. He loved to share his knowledge but didn't want to impose. Eventually, Francie Mae got the chance to ask him her question.

"Cousin Fessor, how did you get out of poverty?" she asked. He paused before thoughtfully answering her question. She and her siblings leaned closer to hear every word. He began slowly as if searching for the right words. He said "I learned that knowledge is power and made plans to get out of poverty by getting an education. Once I got an education, I chose a career to keep me out of poverty. I learned what my rights were and was not afraid to fight for my rights. Some people don't want you to know that," he cautioned.

Her father was self- taught and sought out knowledge. When he could, he read the daily newspapers to keep abreast of current events. Other times, he engaged in long conversations with the men in the community and Cousin Fessor. Like her father, Francie Mae thirsted for knowledge. She volunteered in the school library and had access to all the books she wanted. She had an excellent memory and never tired of seeking answers to her many questions. She and her siblings soaked up information like sponges.

This was also her parent's time to relax and try to distract from the turmoil happening in the world. It was almost too much to bear. Her mother put a big pot of coffee on the stove and the aroma brought a refreshing calm to the room. The engaging conversation continued. This was their safe place to discuss any concerns they had.

Francie Mae learned that everyone has a role to help untangle the web in the fight for equal rights and justice. When everyone is treated equally, everyone can have a chance to succeed. God's intention was for everyone to live peacefully in this world together. To do this, everyone has to pull at the strings. She could pull at the strings by helping to fight for equal rights and getting an education. She made a promise that the civil rights workers fight for justice would not be forgotten. She and others had a big web to untangle.

The Conscience of a Nation

Tippy was now living with relatives in Chicago and attending college at a private university. Vie and Lil Bro was old enough to work part time and contributed to household expenses. Cousin Fessor stayed in touch with Tippy and made frequent visits to Chicago and Ohio to see his children and other cousins. On occasion, Tippy borrowed a relative's car and drove home. Her father had taught her brothers how to respond when stopped by the police but was still worried.

Cousin Fessor told them about the green book for black travelers. Apparently, he and other black people used this book for years. This book was a guide to let black people know where it was safe to stop during their travels. This was necessary because black people, especially men, were subjected to discrimination and threats of violence. There was a list of sundown towns where black people had to be out of town by this time. Cousin Fessor kept a copy of this book and gave a copy to Tippy in case he needed it.

During this time, the civil rights movement and the Vietnam War were still in full swing. Everyone tried to understand what was happening in America. Young men had to register for the draft when they turned eighteen. The thought of going to Vietnam was a constant threat to every young man and their parents. Cousin Fessor said that racial tensions occurred in Vietnam also. Vietnam was the first integrated war. Because of the draft, young black and white men were sent to fight an unpopular war. Some had never interacted with other races. Troops there had to contend with rising tension in the United States as well racially intolerance in a war zone.

Grenades were going off in Vietnam and bombs against black people in our own land. When President Kennedy was assassinated, Francie Mae and her siblings were at school and the principal made an announcement over the intercom. They were stunned. The buses came early to take them home. It seemed like the world stood still. There was a picture of Jesus, Dr. King, and President Kennedy in most black people's kitchens. They all represented hope. They gathered around the pot belly stove for comfort while they discussed what was happening in the land of their birth.

The civil rights movement got stronger. Jim Crow laws made it impossible for most black people to vote. Voting rights activists were killed during Freedom Summer in 1964. Civil rights activists were fighting for the rights of black people throughout the south. Some were killed and some were brutally beaten. Cousin Fessor helped her parents become registered voters. Word spread among the black communities to register to vote and get out and vote. Many people did not have transportation. People with cars volunteered to take people to get registered and to vote. Some black people were fearful of retaliation or didn't think their vote would count.

Some people remembered when residents of Fayette County tried to vote. Fayette County is located near Memphis. Cousin Fessor and her parents remembered. Based on the conversations Francie Mae heard, reportedly, a black man killed a white man and when it was time for trial, no black people were on the jury. They were not allowed to be jurors because they were denied the right to vote. Some white people kept a list of people who registered and they were evicted from their lands. They formed makeshift communities called "Tent Cities". This act drew national attention and was supported by white civil rights activists. People lived in those tents about two years. The U.S. Attorney General Robert F. Kennedy ordered the Justice Department to investigate for civil rights violations. Black people trusted the Kennedy brothers because they seemed to fight for what were right. Cousin Fessor and her parents were determined these cowardly actions would not stop them from voting.

Francie Mae had some knowledge of voting and the rights and responsibilities of citizens. Dad and Cousin Fessor said some politicians were using propaganda and rhetoric to influence others. She didn't know what those big words meant. To make it simple for her, they explained that the politicians knew they were spreading information that was not true but they did it anyway. Some people were easily persuaded due to Southern state laws. Cousin Fessor said it was important to vote so black people and people who wanted to make the world a better place would have political power to make a change.

Black and other poor people were working hard but taxes were not taken out of their paychecks. Farm laborers and others were paid "under the table". This meant there were no earning records for social security benefits. During this time, President Johnson signed into law the Medicare and Medicaid Act and a Food Stamp Act. Finally, Francie Mae and her family finally had health insurance and food stamps to buy food for their hungry stomachs. Because of many injustices, most black people chose a party that supported black people in the fight for economic progress and civil rights.

Francie Mae enjoyed when Cousin Fessor visited. As time passed, they engaged in many conversations about world events. Rom was a history buff and loved to quiz her about what she learned. He looked at her with fire in his light brown eyes when she didn't know the answers. He demanded that she pay attention. "One day you are going to thank me" he said knowingly. As she got older, Lil Bro made sure he told them more and she tried to pay attention. There were so many atrocities against black people that sometimes she got tired of paying attention.

When Cousin Fessor was not around, Lil Bro assisted their father as the historian and was assisted by Rom. She remembered him telling them about hundreds of black people who were murdered in Tulsa, Oklahoma in 1921. A black boy was accused of assaulting a white girl. A riot broke out and the wealthiest black neighborhood in Tulsa was destroyed. Many people were killed. She later learned this was the worst outbreak of racial violence in the United States. She didn't learn about this massacre in school. It seemed like there was no end to these racist stories.

Francie Mae was twelve years old and tired! Like other black children, she was living in a world too hateful for her years. Her parents and Cousin Fessor engaged her siblings and her in honest conversations regarding world events. As a result of these conversations, they appreciated the tireless efforts their ancestors made fighting for equal rights. They were determined to not let them down and become productive citizens.

Hidden Opportunities

The conversations around Pot Belly convinced Francie Mae that hope is not a strategy. Everyone should have hope but can't sit idly around and wait for things to change. Everyone have a role to play in affecting change. The civil rights leaders had hope but they put that hope into action. They had a strategy to achieve major goals.

Francie Mae was convinced hard work has its place but education and knowledge were some of the keys out of poverty. They worked hard in the fields but were still impoverished. Other people worked hard in low wage jobs for other people but were still impoverished. She was an observer of people. Some black people were not impoverished. They were the ones that acquired knowledge, learned a trade and started their own businesses, or pursued a higher level of education. They learned information and skills through experience or formal education. Francie Mae was convinced that no one wants to live in poverty their entire life.

Living in poverty and understanding what was necessary to change her circumstances was the early beginning of her joy and journey out. She had to have goals and a plan. In spite of the dark times, joy became a lifestyle. It was up to her if she wanted it or not. She had a new outlook on life, new tools in her toolbox, and she looked forward to continuing on her journey.

One cold winter day, she went with her father to chop down a pretty evergreen tree for Christmas, he told her the prettiest and largest tree was not always the best tree. They trampled through the woods until they saw the one just for them. She watched as her father grabbed the branch and pulled it toward him. He explained to her that the needles should stay on the tree and shouldn't fall when you shake it. He circled the tree and explained to her that he was looking for bald spots. He told her that you have to know what you are looking for. He told her some trees are diseased so you have to be careful what you choose.

When they took their many walks, he told her to stay on the long narrow road. He warned her not to take shortcuts or take hidden roads. As her father, he knew he couldn't always protect her but gave her the best advice he could. When she became an adult, she had to make decisions for herself. Her parents hoped she would make the right decision. Her father knew that she would make some wrong choices in life but would find her way back to the long narrow road.

One day when her siblings and father weren't around, Francie Mae busied herself by pestering her mother. She knew she was taking a chance but decided to do it anyway. "I'm hungry" she announced to her like this was something new. "Why are we so poor?" she inquired. Her mother swirled around, placed her hands on her hips and looked directly in Francie Mae's now frightened eyes. "Francie Mae, who told you we are poor," she inquired. She wanted to answer that it was obvious but didn't dare part her lips. "It's in your mind" she continued. If it was in her mind, she thought her mind sure didn't tell her growling stomach. "Now stop that foolishness and go outside and play but don't go far. Don't go in the pasture, stay in the front of the house by the tree line", she commanded. Francie Mae knew she meant business so she did as she said.

She ran through the cotton fields in front of their house and didn't stop until she reached the tree line of the woods. She knew that she was under her watchful eyes and felt safe. She played her usual game of make believe. Out of the corner of her eye, she saw a vine filled with juicy blackberries. She crammed those sweet berries in her mouth at rapid speed. When her hunger was satisfied, she made a cup with her hands and brought some berries back to her mother. She found her standing in the kitchen, preparing dinner in the wood burning stove. "I see you found the berries", her mother said. Francie Mae wondered how she knew berries were there. "Francie Mae, everything we need God will provide. You just need to know where to look." Her mother taught her a valuable lesson that she never forgot. This was an opportunity to look in other places for what you need.

Life in the Cotton Fields

When Francie Mae got older she helped her parents and siblings chop and pick cotton. The summer days were long and hot! They were called day labors and met at a designated spot to be picked up by the white overseers' and taken to the fields. In the early morning, they loaded into buses or trucks and were transported to various fields. They stayed days at one field until all the cotton was chopped, then moved on to other fields. Everyone wore straw hats, pants or long skirts, and long sleeves to block the brutal heat from the sun. They packed a paper sack lunch usually containing a bologna sandwich and hoped it would sustain them throughout the long day. After receiving instructions from the overseer, they made sure their hoes were sharp, drank water from the bucket using a community dipper and headed to the beginning of a row.

They stood at the beginning of a row of cotton that seemed approximately a quarter mile long. Their job was to remove the weeds from around the cotton plant. Sometimes the dirt was so hard that their hoes bounced off the ground. Some choppers were able to chop two rolls.

Her parents were some of those choppers. The pay was the same regardless of the number of rows chopped. The choppers wanted to chop two rolls so they could hopefully finish sooner and get out of the scorching field. Francie Mae stuck to one row since she was not experienced. They worked from sun up to sun down. Breaks were limited and there were no toilets. When nature called, they signaled to the overseer and headed to the tree lines to relieve themselves.

As sweat poured from young and old faces, the choppers called "water boy". The little boys stopped playing in the shade nearby and with their little dark arms trembling from the weight, brought a bucket of cool water. The choppers took turns taking a dip of water. At 12 noon, they stopped for lunch. No one wore a watch. Many couldn't afford one. She was taught to tell time by looking at her shadow. When her shadow was short, she knew it was time for everyone to starting walking toward the shade trees for lunch. Sometimes the overseer went to the store to purchase lunch meat, crackers, and a soda for those who could afford it. At the end of the long day, she saw white specks of salt on the backs of some of the choppers. They were dehydrated! This was hard manual labor for three dollars a day!

When the cotton was ready for harvest, usually in late August or early fall, they picked cotton. They lived in Tennessee and there was a compulsory school law. Children couldn't stay out of school to work on the farms. Unlike the white constable who challenged the law with Tippy, these farmers abided by the law. They got to the fields the same way as in chopping cotton. As far as the eye could see, rows of white cotton had burst from the sharp bolls. The cotton was not pretty to Francie Mae since they had to pick it. They were given a long sack with a shoulder strap to put the cotton in and sent on their way. Black and brown hands pulled and twisted the fluffy cotton out of its boll. The bolls are sharp and caused cuts to their gloveless hands. When they got a handful of the fluffy cotton, they put in the sack. They had to bend over to pick the cotton. As they picked, they drug the heavy sack filled with cotton that was strapped to their aching backs.

When the sack was full, they drug the sack to the overseer to be weighed. After weighing, the cotton was loaded on the truck to be transported to the cotton gin. They received their sacks back and start the labor intensive process over again. Francie Mae thought that it was amazing how the human body can be in a stooped position, dragging a heavy sack, filled with cotton, all day. Some pickers became very good, instead of picking one row, they would pick two or three. Eventually this became a competition among them. They would ask one another "How many rows can you carry?" They were not picking cotton for fun; they picked to have money for food, clothes and other necessary essentials. The more cotton picked the more money a person made.

Some workers sang and laughed to break the monotony of the tasks at hand. It was important to have some fun while doing this back breaking work. To Francie Mae, picking cotton was harder than chopping cotton. Her father was considered a good cotton picker and could pick about 400 lbs. of cotton a day. As an extra bonus, or because he was strong and could read and write well, the overseer asked him to go with him to take the cotton to the gin. He earned extra money by doing this. He always came back with treats for Francie Mae and her siblings from the local store. Her father was more educated than the overseer but worked hard in the fields.

Her mother saved the extra money earned, put it in a white handkerchief, and hid it. Her parents had to put some money aside to tide them over in the cold winter months. She tied the handkerchief so tight that only she and Francie Mae could untie it. Francie Mae learned the value of putting money away for what is called a rainy day. You can't spend everything you earn and not consider future needs. Their long term goal was to get out of poverty and remain out of poverty. They were still impoverished but no longer hungry every day.

We Are Soldiers

Throughout her childhood, Francie Mae saw her parents praying but didn't see with her young natural eyes the results of their prayers. She thought that since they lived in poverty, God didn't hear their prayers. What she didn't understand is that poverty is man- made. God intended people to help each other. Church and religious topics did not escape discussion in their family. Historian Lil Bro was happy to lead the discussions. He liked to share the history regarding topics they discussed. He told them that the black church was a safe haven for black men and women to be themselves after the civil war. Religion provided spiritual comfort; therefore most black people had faith in God and went to church.

Religion and church attendance also played a major role in the civil rights movement. In addition to worship, the churches provided a place for the leaders to meet and discuss strategies to fight oppression. Due to racial hatred, some black churches were bombed. So far, in this year alone, Francie Mae knew about seven black and white civil rights workers who were killed and their killers were unknown or tried and freed. The cowardly actions of a small group of racist white people put a blemish on the entire race and the nation. Instead of destroying the souls of black people, they pressed on. Most black people believed that God was a God of justice and in time, these murderers would be punished.

Until now, her parents prayed for her. She was now old enough to pray and make choices for herself. She changed her view. She felt church services were a way for people to come together to praise God, express feelings and provide comfort. There was so much joy inside. She wanted to have this joy in her life. When Francie Mae was twelve years old, she made a decision to be baptized.

Francie Mae remembered hearing the voice of Dr. Martin Luther King over their transistor radio telling people not to despair about the future. Dr. King was a Baptist minister and a civil rights leader. As a preacher, he was a man of faith. A few years earlier, he was jailed for peaceful demonstrations and wrote "Letter from a Birmingham Jail." The letter was to a group of white pastors who wrote a letter in the local newspaper accusing him of disturbing the peace. In his eloquent and thought provoking response, his faith was evident. Many white Christians were indirectly involved in the reign of racial terror by remaining silent. Two years later, she still heard faith, hope and action in his voice over the airwaves. He said that everyone would get to the promised land of racial justice. She had to believe this to be true.

Francie Mae loved going to church. She never knew what would happen but knew it would be exciting and take her mind off the daily struggles of racism and poverty. The pastor of their church did not have a degree in Biblical studies. Like most pastors then, he was called to the ministry by God. As he preached the word, people in the congregation fanned and shouted "Amen". Some women shouted "Preach Passa". In her church, passa was short for pastor. As he continued his sermon, he leaned back and let out loud squawk. The spirit had overtaken him. He stopped for a moment to wipe his sweaty brow with his ever present handkerchief and continued on. Some people "got happy" and jumped in place. Others ran around the sanctuary, raised and waved their hands, and some fainted. What was evident was everyone was praising God.

The ushers walked around the church keeping their eyes on the people shouting. They put their arms around them and fanned them until they calmed down. The choir swayed rhythmically side to side as they song old spirituals. Some of the spirituals dated back to slavery days and offered hope. Prior to church, her mother untied her white tight handkerchief and gave Rom and her a nickel or dime to put in the offering plate. Lil Bro and Vie were now working part time and had their own money.

Francie Mae tried to read her parents old Bible but didn't understand what she was reading. She went to church on Sundays but skipped Sunday school. She thought about what her father and Lil Bro told her years earlier, to think of the Bible as God's story. She wanted to try to understand what she was reading on my own. Lil Bro was a good teacher but he could get philosophical and historical. It took him to long to explain things and she wanted a quick answer.

She gave in and asked her parents. From her understanding, they said the Bible was God's book for people to live by. He speaks to His people through the Bible and helps them to understand the difficult world they live in. God gave them commandments to remember and keep. The people were to love and obey Him and each other. This explanation was good enough for her.

The pastor held revival every fall. To prepare for baptism, she had to sit on the "mourner's bench". Her older siblings and BB were all baptized and now it was her turn. During revival, a group of children were directed to the front benches by the church ushers. Family members and other church members sat in the pews and prayed and sang for them. The boys sat on hard benches on one side of the church and the girls on the opposite side. These benches were called "the mourner's bench". They had to sit on those hard benches since they were mourners and sinners seeking salvation. They were dressed in their Sunday best while the children patiently waited for the spirit of God to come upon them.

The pastor of the church preached fiery sermons as usual. He spoke about sin and fearing God. The old deacons got down on one knee, put their hands on their bowed heads, and prayed for souls. The ushers and mothers of the church were dressed in white uniforms and wore white gloves on their hands. Their thick cotton stockings were rolled up to their knees. The deacons and mothers prayed and sang hymns until the mourners jumped off the bench, shouted and confessed they had accepted Jesus as their Savior. After a child jumped up, many people in the congregation shouted also. Revival went on for a week at a time and often late into the night. After one child jumped up, another jumped up. One by one, children jumped off the bench. If a child didn't "get off the bench" during revival that year, there was a year's wait until the next revival.

Francie Mae sat on the cold hard bench every night during revival that year. Her parents were praying for her. She didn't remember her siblings jumping up a few years earlier but remembered when BB jumped off the bench and started crying and raising her arms. Francie Mae wondered what was wrong with her that the spirit didn't touch her and make her jump up and shout. She was one of the last children on the bench. The deacons and mothers continued to pray for her sinful soul. Secretly she wondered if the spirit didn't touch her because she didn't go to Sunday school. She was concerned and as usual, asked her parents. They told her that the spirit of God touches people in different ways. Some were silent and some expressive. All she had to do was believe in Jesus.

Before revival ended the next night, she remembered what her parents told her. All she had to do was believe and she would be saved. She didn't remember reading in the Bible that she had to shout. She believed so she rose from that bench with tears in her eyes and went to the pulpit to confess her belief to the pastor so she could be baptized.

At the end of the revival, all the new believers stood on the pulpit with the pastor and were introduced to the congregation. While standing on the pulpit she heard an old lady in the congregation sing a hymn called "We Are Soldiers". She was old in years but her voice was strong and powerful. The old lady had her eyes closed and was swaying in her seat. Her weathered face told a story that she had a hard life but her faith never wavered. She struggled to stand. The person sitting next to her had to help her up. She raised her crooked index finger and said "Passa I got a word for the children". Apparently, she was one of the oldest members of the church. She told them that every Christian was called to be a soldier in the army of God. She said soldiers are called to fight, love God and conquer evil. Her voice turned into a loud shout before she took her seat.

She closed her eyes again and starting back singing and swaying. The converts knew the song so the pastor asked them and the rest of the congregation to join. Swaying rhythmically side to side and clapping their hands to the beat, they lifted their voices and sang.

"We are Soldiers,

In the army,

We have to fight although we have to cry
We have to hold up the blood stained banner,
We have to hold it up until we die"!

They sang all verses of this powerful song. Tears streamed down their young faces. Lil Bro and Vie sang in the choir in school and learned about music. Francie Mae found out that this song was written by an unknown person in the 1880's. It was often song in black churches as a hymn and by civil rights leaders when they marched for equality.

About a week later, the new converts were baptized in a small muddy pond on the church's property. They wore white gowns and the girls wore white head scarves or swimming caps to keep their hair in place. One by one, the deacons lead them into the pond to be baptized. Prior to dipping us in the muddy water, the pastor told them that water baptism didn't save them; it was the blood of Jesus who died for them. Francie Mae made the most important decision of her life. This was the beginning of her Christian walk out of poverty. She had to learn how to help untangle the web the right way.

Enjoy the Adventure

A squirrel stopped and looked at Francie Mae before scurrying up the hard brown bark of the oak tree. He was in search of acorns to feed his family. On the other side of the tree, a spider was building its web in the overgrown weeds. He was hoping Francie Mae didn't disturb the web he was building to trap bugs to eat. Francie Mae did not see the squirrel or the spider. She was still dreaming, learning about her history and trying to figure out how to untangle the web.

It was many years before Francie Mae and her family was able to move from shacks and into a stable house. They did not have electricity or indoor plumbing but they had each other and good neighbors. Currently, they lived in a place called "The Bottom". The bottom was about a two mile long gravel curved road filled with families living in shacks. There was a name for the road but everyone just called it "The Bottom". It curved downhill to the low land filled with cotton. Approximately ten of the poorest families lived on this road. Overtime, all the shacks had electricity except theirs. They did not have money to pay the electric bill.

Francie Mae's elementary school years were the start of planning for short and long term goals. Her parents insisted they continue to study, not miss school, be obedient and do their best. The bus drivers, teachers and principals were invested in the students. During school hours, the teachers were the adults that spent the majority of time with them. They were all black and did not live in poverty. There had to be a reason they didn't. They became her mentors and she was determined to learn from them.

The nurturing principal, assistant principal and teachers treated all students the same. They believed they could excel and wanted them to believe also. Every year, they looked forward to the beautiful pageant held in the gymnasium. It was magically transformed into a fairy land. Students from each class participated in dances honoring their country and other countries. These dances were taught to perfection by her teachers. Various pageant wagons were elaborately decorated and glided slowing across the polished gym floor. The pageant queen wore a beautiful white dress with a crown perched on top of her curls. She looked like a princess. She and her court of equally elaborately dressed girls and boys were on the last pageant wagon. Francie Mae gasped in awe watching the beauty of it all. The teachers, principals, students and parents worked long hours as a team to make this an enjoyable and memorable event. They lived during a time of so much oppression that they wanted the students to have happiness and beauty in their memory.

The students had to raise money to become the pageant queen or member of the court. One way of raising money was to sell chocolate chip or oatmeal cookies. The teachers counted a certain number of cookies, and placed them in a brown paper bag to give to the students to sell. They sent a note home to the children's parents about the fund raiser. The parents had to sign the note before the students could participate. Her parents didn't sign the notes she brought home but she wanted to participate. One girl on her bus was successful in selling the top number of cookies almost every year and was the pageant queen. Francie Mae didn't care about being the queen; she just wanted dance and ride on the pageant wagon.

One day after she presented her case, one of her parents signed the note. She took the signed note back to school and got her bag of oatmeal cookies to sell. On the long bus ride home, she did not ask a single student to buy cookies from her. The smell of the cookies penetrated through the bag and she resisted the urge to eat one. Many children stuck their heads out of the bus window to feel the breeze or because they bored of the ride.

She stood up and stuck her head out of the bus window hoping that she would no longer smell the sweet aroma of the cookies.

Around mile marker eight, hunger pangs got the best of her. She took one cookie from the stapled brown paper bag and placed it in her mouth. Other children on the bus were also overcome with hunger pangs. They couldn't afford to buy cookies so she passed a few out to them. By the time she got home, her stained brown paper bag was empty. There were no cookies and no crumbs. Her mother looked knowingly at her and asked to see the bag of cookies. Francie Mae couldn't make up an excuse because by the look in her mother's eyes, she knew the truth. Plus, she didn't realize the cookie crumbs were all around her mouth!

She was so ashamed of disappointing her parents. They trusted her to sell the cookies but she ate them. Her mother wrote a note to send to the teacher explaining what she done. Her parents spent their hard earned money to pay for what Francie Mae took. They didn't want to sign the notes because they knew to never give a hungry child cookies to sell. They gave in because they didn't want her to feel left out. Francie Mae's punishment was to apologize to the teacher, do extra chores at home and during her free time at school. The teachers understood that many children were hungry but they didn't want any child to feel left out either. They probably paid for many cookies.

Francie Mae's task at school was to work in the school library and help the teachers decorate the bulletin boards. She discovered her love of books while serving out her punishment. She was able to take adventures and journeys anywhere she wanted. Her mind was occupied with thoughts other than oppression and hunger. She redeemed herself so the librarian let her check out books to take home. She escaped into her own world. Almost every day, she read chapters from a book. As she got more involved in reading *Little Women*, she began to question life as she knew it. The main female characters in the book were sisters. They were feisty, poor, fun loving, kindhearted and along with their mother, helped their poor neighbors. Their father was away serving in the military during the civil war. The sisters found their special place in the world after they grew up. They just didn't accept life as it was and helped untangle the web. She decided that she wouldn't accept life as it was either. She continued her journey in the world of books and enjoyed each adventure.

After working in the library for the rest of the year, she redeemed herself. The next year, she was chosen to participate in the class dance honoring various countries. She and her classmates practiced snapping their fingers to the beat of the music. They danced until the clack of their shoes on the wooden gym floor signaled they were all in step. While listening to the music and dancing, she temporarily forgot her hunger and impoverished life. The teachers chipped in to buy material and made their beautiful costumes so their parents didn't have to pay.

Francie Mae learned her lesson. When she took the cookies, she felt bad. She vowed to never take anything that wasn't hers again. Taking things that didn't belong to her did not untangle the web. She had to contribute by pulling a string.

Period of Awakening

    While napping, Francie Mae had drifted from the big trunk of the oak tree and was now lying on the grassy ground beneath. Her unruly hair had found its way from their braids and was now a clump of curls. She knew her mother would call her if she stayed outside too long. She had to hurry and finish her dream of information.

    Her period of awakening happened while living impoverished. As she learned more about the history of the American flag, National Anthem and the United States Constitution during elementary school, her why start turning into what. She was tired of asking why they were in poverty. Now it was time to ask what they could do to get out. She learned more about her rights and why brave civil rights leaders were risking their lives to fight for civil rights. She was behind the starting line but was determined to make a strong finish.

Her short term goals were to obey her parents, be observant, listen and learn, get baptized, attend church on a regular basis, study hard, earn good grades and learn from her teachers and principals. They became her mentors. In spite of different laws, they were educated, employed, and lived in stable housing. They were nurturing and had a passion for what they did. Apparently they chose the right occupations to keep them employed. They did it so it could be done! She learned that faith, education and steady employment were some passages to progress.

She had to change the way she viewed the different laws and poverty. Just because some other people thought black people would be poor didn't mean she had to. Just because some other people thought black people should live by different laws didn't mean it was right. She had to have a different view of things so she could help untangle the web. She changed her mindset.

She came to realize that God did not forget about them. Like the good figs, HE put them in a community and placed trustworthy people in their lives as living examples of what they could become. She knew that people were not made to go through life alone. She learned that as people journey through life, there are many difficulties. There are opportunities in every difficulty. The long dirt road Francie Mae lived on was filled with holes when it rained. They had to walk about two miles to go to the grocery store. In the summer, there were no trees on the road to protect them from the sun. After walking up and down the road many times, the walk got easier. Like the long dirt road they lived on, difficult roads can help build character and appreciation of a beautiful life.

Francie Mae believed in her parents. They lived together every day and she observed their behavior. They were her living examples. In spite of economic hardships and racial oppression, they remained hopeful. Her father served honorably in WWII and was not able to get meaningful employment to provide for his family. In spite of this, he always had a friendly smile, had kind words to share with people, and looked for other opportunities. Her mother was his source of strength and support. They had standards for their home and did not allow negative influences or behaviors to occupy the family's space.

She learned that there were some people who wanted to help untangle the web. The web was hard to untangle because of old beliefs that people didn't want to change. The racial oppression they experienced as a black family did not represent the opinions of the majority of people. People are influenced by negative behavior or positive behavior. Sometimes it's easier to sway to the negative and give up. Her parents never gave up and chose the positive behavior. They had a positive mindset and mentality. They were giving Francie Mae and her siblings the best gift for success. They didn't allow their circumstances to define them.

Bloom Where You're Planted

With a swift move of her hand, Francie Mae brushed her long unruly hair from her face. The leaves of the oak tree continued to provide protection. The squirrel lost interest in her a long time ago. As long as she didn't disturb the bug in its web, the spider was content. The cool breeze continued to blow across her face so she drifted back off to sleep.

Francie Mae enjoyed the wide open spaces of the outdoors. It was the perfect place to be alone and think. Naps were the best when taken outdoors under the comfort of the big tree. Her big sister Vie preferred to stay inside. Her hair was always adorned with pretty hair barrettes. She learned how to sew in school and made pretty skirts. Francie Mae thought she looked like a princess. Vie enjoyed helping their mother prepare food to cook. Francie Mae liked helping in the garden but had no patience for learning to cook. One day, Vie made her a pretty orange flared skirt with the material she got from school. Francie Mae loved the swishing sound the skirt made when she danced. Vie used scraps of cloth to make colorful curtains for the broken windows in the shack. She made a flower bed in the front yard and planted flowers that rivaled an artist's palette. The shack was looking like a warm and beautiful home.

When Francie Mae got older, her father taught her to chop wood with an axe. They needed firewood to put into the potbelly stove. After her father and brothers brought the wood to the woodpile, they selected the best piece to put on the chopping block. Her father taught her that every piece of wood had a fat end and a thin end. He started from the top, raised his sharp axe over his head, and with a downward force, split the wood down the middle. When it was hunting season, her father, Lil Bro, Rom and the man who lived in the next shack went rabbit hunting in the nearby woods. Francie Mae wanted to go but her father wouldn't let her.

When it was fishing season she helped her mother and the neighbor lady dig in the ground for worms for bait. They put them in a tin can with dirt, and went fishing. They used a pole rigged with a fishing hook and bobber and went to the "fishing hole". They baited the hook with the wiggly worms and waited for the fish to bite. When the plastic bobber moved, they knew a fish was at the other end. They yanked the pole out of the water and put the fish in a tin pail. This was their dinner! They learned that word of mouth was the way to find the best fishing holes. When they heard the "fish was biting" at a different fishing hole they trekked through the woods with their straw hats, and long sleeves. Sometimes they had to wait a long time for the fish to bite. They found the wait to be relaxing. They were enjoying nature and temporarily forget about the daily struggles.

They adjusted to their new surroundings but it was difficult. There was too much turmoil in the United States, especially the south. Many of their neighbors hunted and farmed in addition to working other jobs. They shared what they had with other families in need. This is how she met her best friend BB. She and her family lived on the main road, owned their own home and had tasty apple and peach trees in the backyard. The children and adults became friends. She learned the value of friendship. Until they moved to "The Bottom," they never lived close enough to their neighbors to meet them. She was not lonesome because she had siblings but never knew how it felt to love and trust someone outside of her family.

Her friend BB was a year older than Francie Mae and was a grade higher. They had similar interests. She liked to dance also. She learned to pop her fingers to the lively songs she heard over the transistor radio. They lived about two miles from each other but visited each other like they lived next door. They enjoyed the long walks to and from each other's house. There was always something to talk about. When it was time to go home, they walked each other "piece way" and laughed and talked the entire distance. Since the road was so long, they had a special place picked out to say their temporary goodbyes before starting their journey back home.

Francie Mae and her sibling's friends didn't seem to notice or care that they were poor and lived in a shack. They just enjoyed the fun times they had together. They also had similar interests. Lil Bro and BB's oldest brother enjoyed playing basketball until it was too dark to see. Vie and BB's oldest sister was both talkative and enjoyed trying different hairstyles. Rom and BB's other brother both enjoyed talking about and working on cars. This was a true example of friendship.

Because they didn't have a television, Francie Mae and her siblings spent many Saturday's at BB and her family's house watching variety shows on their small black and white TV. As she got older, she became socially aware and looked forward to seeing black people in other non-stereotypical roles. She saw a television show about a beautiful widowed black nurse with a small son. She worked in an office with a friendly white doctor. They were living in an apartment complex with friendly white neighbors. The show was named "Julia" and Diahann Carroll was the beautiful actress that played the title role. One episode was about downsizing in the office. The clinic manager wanted to downsize Julia's position since she was a minority. The white doctor objected to this decision and intervened on her behalf. He reminded the clinic manager that this was a violation of the Civil Rights Act. The rights of black people and other people of color were addressed on national television in a sitcom. Someone in a position to stand up for injustice did so and the result was a positive outcome. This helped untangle the web.

One day she got a chance to see her favorite singer on a variety show and was in awe of his fancy dance moves and showmanship. Francie Mae couldn't wait to get home to imitate his dance moves. She grabbed the old straw broom for a microphone, spun around and dropped to her knees. When she got up, blood was dripping from her skinned knees. She was too excited to feel the pain. Instead, she laughed out loud because it felt so good to dance and relieve stress.

Francie Mae and her family didn't have extra money to go shopping for clothes. Most of the time, she wore clothes that were "handed down". This meant the clothes were worn by someone else. One day, Francie Mae, BB and their mothers went on a shopping spree. They had to dress just right for the occasion. They put on their straw hats, long sleeves and instead of a purse, carried a stick with a nail in the bottom. They walked through the woods until they got to a place called "the dump". This was nothing but a landfill where well to do people discarded unwanted clothes and household items. They spent hours bearing the stench to find the perfect articles of clothing and other items. After bringing their treasures home, her mother put the clothes in pans on the potbelly stove and boiled them until they were clean. She hung them on the clothes line to dry. After drying, she heated the old iron on the same potbelly stove and ironed the clothes to perfection.

As Francie Mae continued on her difficult journey, she learned to value friends and appreciate life. She was determined to help improve their circumstances and help others along the way. They suffered economically but not spiritually or emotionally. They learned to adapt to temporary conditions and not lose hope. Like the beautiful flowers Vie planted in the front yard, she learned to bloom where she was planted.

The Oak Tree

Francie Mae stirred slightly but didn't wake up from her long nap. Her dream took her a few years back in time. The cool breeze touched her face and neck. The green leaves of the big tree swayed in the wind. Francie Mae continued to nap underneath its protective leaves. This was her favorite place to read. The oak tree was her symbol of strength, endurance and liberty. The oak tree leaf is a powerful symbol and is a symbol of rank in the United States armed forces.

Francie Mae and her family were living in a small friendly military community near Memphis. The small downtown area was populated with a large grocery store, businesses, doctor's office, retail shops, tattoo shops and a movie theatre. There was a large elementary and high school located in the town but only white students could attend. To get to downtown Memphis, they rode the local city bus pass the sprawling Naval Base and the beautiful large school with the invisible sign of whites only.

When they passed the Navy Base, she was intrigued by the service people who were dressed smartly in their uniforms and was curious about their stories. As she peered out the windows of the bus she saw the lively activities of people living life. She didn't see "colored" or "white" signs like she did in the big city. What she saw were groups of people of different ages and races getting along. They seemed to have a common goal.

There were bus stops in front of the Navy Base. The Sailors, Marines and other people got on the bus and rode to Memphis. Black and white service people sat together and talked and laughed all the way to their destinations. Other people on the bus did the same.

They had to pass a housing project on their way to downtown. The housing project was located on both sides of a busy city street. She looked on both sides and saw rows of beautiful brick apartment style homes with green lawns. Young white children played outside while white adults were busy going about their day. She made up her mind that she would live in one of those brick homes one day.

As the years passed, Francie Mae learned to spell well. Every night, she practiced her spelling words by the dim light of the coal-oil lamp. Toward the end of the year, her fifth grade teacher lined the students up on each side of the room, girls against boys for a spelling match. The two top winners received a shiny quarter. It was just enough money to buy lunch and milk. If the students didn't have a lunch or lunch money, they did without. The teacher knew she would always place first or second and this was her way of letting Francie Mae earn lunch money. She didn't want to single any student out and make them feel ashamed. Francie Mae won a quarter to eat lunch. Almost every day, she gave her shiny quarter to the motherly cafeteria lady and enjoyed a healthy lunch.

The next year, the spelling competition continued. She was now in sixth grade with a new teacher. Her new teacher followed the same process. More students practiced their spelling words for a chance of winning the shiny quarter. Again, she always came in first or second and the teacher reached in his pocket and handed her a shiny quarter. One day, her winning streak ended. A new teacher began teaching at the school and her son was her classmate. There were now three top spellers. She was the hungriest of the three and studied harder for her spot. One day, he came in first, the other girl came in second and she was third. She was crushed!

The rules of the game changed. The teacher told them that the four top spellers would have an opportunity to work in the serving line of the cafeteria. Francie Mae got an instant job working in the cafeteria serving lunch to her fellow students. Under the watchful eyes of the motherly cafeteria ladies, they were taught food safety and hygiene. One of the ladies showed her how to wear her long curly unruly hair under the mandatory hair net. After serving, they ate lunch free. She spent more time studying her spelling words for fear she would lose her job and free lunch. Serving others gave her a good feeling and she learned what responsibility felt like. This was her first job outside the cotton field and it felt great.

When she got home, she ran to the old oak tree to tell him her thoughts. "Oak tree, one day I will no longer be poor. I am going to study harder, and get a job helping others. I am going to wear an oak tree leaf so I can remember you forever," she exclaimed. The green leaves on the oak tree swayed in the cool breeze. A branch swayed down near her as if to listen closer. The old oak tree never tired of listening to her ideas.

Earning Her Own Money

Francie Mae knew her secrets were safe with the protective old oak tree. This was why under the tree was her favorite spot to read and nap. By this time, she had napped for about an hour.

Francie Mae's two oldest brothers, Tippy and Lil Bro were gifted artists and took art in school. She could draw some things but was by no means an artist. She had a plan. She made sure her elementary age classmates knew her brothers were artists. Since Lil Bro went to the same school, some had seen his artistic abilities but not Tippy's.

She asked them both to draw a picture to take to school to show her classmates. She asked Lil Bro for some of his art paper. Using their skills as leverage, she decided to draw paper dolls and sell them to her classmates for three cents. She drew two pieces of clothes for each doll for three cents more. She decided on three cents since parents gave their children three cents for milk at school. Since most girls wanted the paper doll and her clothes, they were willing to do without milk, save and pay the extra three cents.

In case her spelling gig didn't last she had to have another option. She became quite the entrepreneur until her mother found out. Her mother wanted to know how she was getting this money. After Francie Mae told her and showed her the inventory to prove it, she made her stop. She was crushed. Her mother told her that the other children were poor also. The money they gave her for paper dolls was meant for milk. Like her, they didn't have extra money to spend.

In the summer, Francie Mae returned to working long days in the cotton field. On some weekends, she went downtown with her father to "eye buy" since they didn't have much money to spend. One day, she saw a beautiful watch displayed in the window of the local five and dime store. It was a Timex Alice in Wonderland watch with a blue band. She was determined to buy that watch. She was eleven years old and tired of getting things other people didn't want. She wanted something new and had an idea on how to get it.

When she went to the field again, she approached the overseer about her idea. She asked to sharpen the other workers hoes. Her father taught her the art of hoe sharpening and she was fast and efficient. A sharp hoe was crucial to making sure all the weeds were removed from the cotton plants and made the job easier. This was a win for both the workers and the overseer. The workers were able to get back to the field and chop quicker and the overseer knew the cotton plants would grow better. This earned her an extra quarter a day. If she sharpened hoes for thirty days, she could buy that watch! The first time she got a quarter, she held it in her sweaty hand all day. She was determined to be a good steward over her earnings. At the end of the summer, her father took her downtown again and there it was, still waiting for her! She handed the friendly clerk her hard earned quarters. She made her first purchase with her own money!

The watch served as a constant reminder that she had to work for what she wanted. Sometimes you have to create your own jobs. She worked hard, got tired, but kept her eyes on the prize. She learned by paying attention and observing; a person could recognize a need and create a way to make money by fulfilling the need.

By this time, she and her family had lived almost twelve years in economic poverty but she was a happy child. Her parents were positive living examples for their children. She learned money is necessary to buy basic needs but she had to take care of the money she earned. This meant that she had to save some of her money. She worked many long hours to earn money to buy that watch and had to take care of it. She got joy from working, earning money, and saving money.

As she continued on her journey, she learned many more valuable lessons in life. As she grew, her value system grew. Things that seemed important to other people became less important to her. It was more important to love and respect people. The heart of people has to change so they can help untangle the web.

The Long Road

One day as Francie Mae walked with her father on the long gravel road from "The Bottom", they discussed their career ambitions. She was nearing her teen years old but still enjoyed walking and talking with her father. He was a man of faith, insightful and a very wise man who was displaced in the south. He still enjoyed writing editorials for The Commercial Appeal, the local newspaper. One day, his editorial was selected for publication. He wrote about how the white led labor unions and racist politicians in Memphis barred non-professional black people from obtaining meaningful employment. All men wanted to provide for their families and black men were no exception. He wrote that he was excluded from meaningful work after being honorably discharged from the Army and he was still being excluded. It was 1965 and he was discharged twenty two years previously.

As they walked, Francie Mae shared that one day, she wanted to live in one of those beautiful brick apartments that she saw from the bus while riding to Memphis. Her father smiled at her and with a twinkle in his light brown eyes; he told her that was a possibility. One of the white civilian employers in Human Resources at the Navy Base read his editorial and wrote him a letter. During those times, when a letter to the editor was published, the name and address was also published. The man asked her father to come in for an interview. He was selected to attend an eight week training program under the Manpower Development and Training Act of 1962 to become a custodian. This federal program was created by President John F. Kennedy and approved by Congress. The training site was in Memphis and he was given a training allowance, additional pay for dependents, and a transportation allowance. Her father completed training and was hired as a custodian in the Non-Commissioned Officers (NCO) Club. He was fifty nine years old when he obtained his first job with a steady paycheck and benefits. Francie Mae was so proud of her brave father!

A chain of events took place. Her father continued to have faith and wrote a powerful letter to the local newspaper. His article was read by a hiring manager with a kind heart who saw beyond race. He helped untangle the web.

After her father starting working at the Base, over the years, Lil Bro, Vie and Rom were able obtain summer employment on the base since they were still in school. Lil Bro and Rom bought their first used cars. Rom was interested in auto mechanics and changed high schools to one that offered this trade. Sometimes they worked extra shifts to help pay for the cars. Ron drove his light blue car to and from school. He still had to drive by the all-white high school to a school located closer to Memphis. Tinkering under the hood of the car kept him busy for hours. Like most children, growing up living in poverty and racism affected him. He was quick to anger and this was a good outlet for his pent-up emotions.

Lil Bro and Vie graduated from high school while they lived in "The Bottom". Lil Bro was drafted and was serving as a Military Police in the Army. He became a paratrooper to earn extra money. George was still in Chicago attending college. Since he was in college, he was given a student deferment. Due to financial difficulties later, he had to work and he dropped below the required hours of study for a deferment. He was re-classified and, was drafted by the Army. Upon advice of his white professor, he went to the Air Force recruiting station with the intent of applying for flight training. He passed the rigorous test and was accepted into the Air Force. After being sworn in and completing his medical examination, it was determined he had astigmatism. He could not apply to flight school.

Instead, because of his high scores, he received a top security clearance and served four years in military intelligence.

Vie graduated from business school in Memphis and moved to a town about eighty miles away to work as a secretary for a white college professor at a black college. There, she met a college student who was a former sailor, and later got married. The next year, she announced they were expecting a bundle of joy! Francie Mae was overjoyed and was looking forward to being an Aunt. She was fourteen years old, in ninth grade and pondering her own future.

Since Francie Mae's birth, numerous civil rights leaders, workers, and anyone who stood for justice or equality were assassinated or killed in another manner. The list included black and white people. Some made the national news, others didn't. In February 1965, Malcolm X, American Muslim minister and human rights activist, was murdered in New York.

On April 4, 1968, Dr. Martin Luther King was assassinated in her hometown of Memphis. He came to Memphis to lead the Memphis Sanitation Worker's Strike. People throughout the nation reacted with shock and grief to his murder. It seemed like Francie Mae's heart stopped along with his. His death touched off a wide rampage of rioting across the nation. Rioting was not right but people were emotional. Some people took to the street, smashing store windows and setting fires. There were mandatory curfews in place. Army and National Guard Troops were on duty throughout the nation.

A few days after Dr. King's death, his courageous widow, held a press conference encouraging people to remember what her husband stood for. Prior to his funeral, she and her three oldest children flew to Memphis and led The Silent Memorial March in his honor. There were over twenty thousand marchers and people lining the streets. Francie Mae and her father rode the bus to Memphis to participate in this peaceful march. National Guardsmen lined the streets and helicopters circled overhead. Black and white people marched along in unity, young and old. It was a humbling experience.

In June of the same year, another ally for civil rights, Senator Robert F. Kennedy was assassinated in Los Angeles while campaigning for U.S. President. After his brother, President John F. Kennedy, was assassinated years earlier, he was the most popular white politician to be supported by black people. He showed sensitivity to the plight of black people by rebuilding slums, feeding the hungry, providing job opportunities and advocating for peace in Vietnam. His campaign slogan was "Kennedy for a Better America." Senator Kennedy backed aspirations for poor people, poor black people and other people of color. Black and white people were left in sorrow and tears again. These politicians, civil rights leaders and workers, and other people were trying to help untangle the web.

One day as Francie Mae and her father enjoyed their brisk walk; she thought about the ongoing injustice and violence in the world and got angry. Again, she was surprised by her own emotions. She was tired of the racism, discrimination, demonstrations, marches, rioting, bombings, violence and assassinations. She was fourteen years old and wondered when it would all end. More organizations were formed to fight for justice and equality. This life was all she knew and it began to suck the life out of her.

Because black people were different in appearance, some white people justified their different treatment of them. People carry the color they were born with for life. She didn't understand why black people were judged on skin color, not abilities. Black people were tired of the injustices and pained by the constant fear of living while black. Civil right protests shifted from the south to the north and west. Riots and violence broke out all over the nation.

Francie Mae had lived a long fourteen years and felt robbed of her childhood. Black children were affected by the racial turmoil across the nation. This was a painful way to live. It seemed that every time someone was courageous enough to fight for the cause of black and poor people, they were beaten or killed.

Senator Kennedy wanted to overhaul the draft system to eliminate bias like student deferments. Most black students were not in college or if they were, struggling to keep the required number of hours to avoid the draft. Senator Kennedy wanted to end student deferments because it favored the wealthy. More young black men were on the front lines in Vietnam while more young white men were in college.

She thought about the safety of her brothers who were drafted and now serving in the military. This was another fear to add to her long list of fears. Some years earlier, her sixteen year old first cousin went missing and was never heard from again. He was trying to find a job as a day laborer. He was reported as missing but the police refused to investigate.

As they walked, her father listened to her rantings and paused to gather his thoughts before he asked her this question. "Do you know what faith is?" She knew what the Bible said faith was and gave him the memorized Biblical response but didn't know what it really meant. He didn't seem impressed with her response. With a firm voice that's usually not firm, he said, "As long as we live in this world, we will have difficult times. True faith is having the confidence that God will see you through. You can't say you have faith then stop when you're tired. You have to continue to fight for equal justice. " He obviously felt the need to make sure she understood what he was saying to her before continuing. He told her that when they moved to the community seven years ago, they were strangers in the community and didn't know the road or what to expect. He looked down on the road they were walking on and told her the road was long and the walk was tiring. He said they needed groceries from the store on the highway so the only way to get there was to walk the long road.

Speaking like a soldier, he said their mission was to get to the store and back. Over the years, the long walk didn't seem so long because they got used to it. They had a different approach to accomplish their mission. Instead of the road being tiring, they learned to appreciate the peace. With peace, they had time to think and plan. No one drove down the roads and called them derogatory names.

He told her the civil right workers and leaders were also tired but kept their faith. He said that everyone can help in the fight for justice and social equality. He warned her to not let her emotions get the best of her or her mind won't process what it needs to. He wanted her to understand that on a just road, there are no shortcuts. He pointed out that there are shortcuts to go somewhere else but it won't lead to where you want to go. He paused again for effect. "Do you understand what I am saying to you, he asked?" She answered affirmatively so he continued. He told her that some roads are hidden and if she took the hidden road, she may get lost. He told her that people will try to lead another person astray and count on their emotional state to make the wrong decision and take a shorter road.

When Francie Mae thought he had made his point, he continued. His voice changed from firmness back to gentleness. He told her that there is no way they can control events that happen in the nation but had to continue to fight and believe in hope. He wanted her to know the work the civil rights workers are giving their life for should mean something. He told her to not let anyone get inside her mind and cause confusion. He advised that if it takes a long road to get her safely to the right place, take that long road. If she had faith and put in the work, she would achieve. By this time, they had traveled the long road from their shack to the grocery store on the highway.

Her father's job as a custodian at the Naval Base was their stepping stone to moving on up. One day, she went with him to look for houses in Memphis. They rode the city bus from Millington to Memphis and walked in various neighborhoods looking for houses. By this time, she knew the beautiful brick apartment homes were actually located in housing projects and considered a ghetto. This did not matter to her because they were not shacks. They were brick, had electricity and indoor plumbing. If they could just move to the city, she knew eventually, they move to that housing project.

With her parent's nurturing and firm guidance, Francie Mae learned to live life to the fullest. She decided that no one gets to choose how she lives it. She continued to volunteer in the school library because it helped counteract the angry feelings she had. It also gave her a sense of purpose. She remembered reading in one of the insightful books that a person has to free themselves. Freedom moves from the inside out. It started with her. This was another step in her escape from oppression to opportunity.

Her parents could only pray and trust that their children would continue to take the long road, avoid shortcuts and hidden roads. She was prepared to be resilient so she learned how to bump along the long rough road. She figured it wouldn't last forever.

The National Housing Act (NHA) was developed to make buying houses more affordable. The purpose was to improve housing standards and help end crime ridden slums. The problem was that only white people benefited. As part of this act, loan corporations created a color coded system called Redlining to determine what neighborhoods would be viable for loans and mortgages. Black neighborhoods were coded red for high risk. Banks denied loans and mortgages because of the perceived risk. Without finances, homes and neighborhood buildings fell into disrepair.

Prior to the beginning of her tenth grade year, she and her family moved from "The Bottom" back to Memphis. She was now a poverty veteran and thought it couldn't get worse. She transitioned from absolute poverty to a different type of poverty. Life in the ghetto was different from life in a rural farming community.

White flight occurred when white people moved out of urban areas that were more racially diverse to suburban areas. Some white people were afraid to live around people who didn't look like them or were poor. Black and white poor families had no choice but to live in urban areas that were defunded. White real estate investors, property owners and land developers found a new way around anti-discriminatory policies. There were still secret practices like blockbusting. This practice persuaded property owners to sell cheaply because they feared people of other races or classes would move into the neighborhood. After the white families moved, developers sold the properties to black people at double the cost. Many homes were rent to own. Black homeowners had a hard time keeping their property up because the cost was too high and they couldn't get loans. As a result, they lost their homes and the developers started the same scheme over. This contributed to a never ending cycle of poverty. This practice was outlawed with the Civil Rights Act of 1968 but the damage was already done.

Various ways were found to keep black people and poor white people in low income and segregated areas. Laws were changed but people found ways to get around the laws. This was not fair and didn't feel right. When laws are changed, people should be held accountable.

The road out of poverty can be a long process. It takes everyone to admit there are problems, and work together to find a common ground that will benefit everyone. Everyone can pull at strings to untangle the web.

Leveling the Playing Field

Francie Mae enjoyed hearing stories from her parents. They tried to explain things in ways her young mind could understand. They talked about race and race relations. They taught her to succeed in life, a person must want to. Sometimes barriers would be in the way but she had to remove them.

When Francie Mae's mother was a little girl, she used to play baseball. She explained that a baseball game is played between two teams and there are rules of the game. Each team takes a turn at bat. It didn't matter how far behind a team falls behind in a game; they had time to come back.

People of color and poor people needed to have a turn at bat. Because of unequal laws, they needed time to come back. Francie Mae dreamed of a time when everyone had equal rights. People wanted jobs that paid living wages, had benefits, and fair and stable housing. She and other poor children were tired of living with hunger and in shacks. They wanted to go to neighborhood schools instead of being bused long distances to low funded schools.

Living in stable housing, having food to eat and medical care are basic human rights. Prior to the Medicare and Medicaid program of 1965, these basic needs were not met for black and poor people. The civil rights workers were trying to fix these barriers called systemic racism and have a turn at bat. Eventually, Francie Mae and her family received help from government programs.

When laws changed, Francie Mae and her family were able to move from shacks to a beautiful housing project in the city. This was the same project she saw from the windows of the bus years ago. She was almost fifteen years old and this was the first time she and her family had electricity and indoor plumbing. They had food, stable housing and health insurance. They had warmth from the cold winters and cool relief from the sweltering summers. The people living there were also poor but there were no cotton fields. The cotton fields were replaced by views of hospitals and downtown. She learned that initially, black people were not allowed to live in this housing project. There was a movement called white flight. When white people left the downtown area to move to the suburbs, black people moved into homes they vacated.

Francie Mae attended a beautiful new high school that was within walking distance of her new home. The students were from lower middle class and lower income families. A few white students attended the same school. The students were all eager to learn and determined to succeed. The teachers and principals were of all races and backgrounds. They were all determined to help the students achieve.

Her high school years were filled with excitement. It felt good to walk to a neighborhood school instead of riding approximately thirty two miles round trip on a school bus. She enjoyed social relationships and joined various clubs. She still enjoyed reading books and volunteered to work in the school library. Many students volunteered to work in various capacities. Volunteering was a great way to meet people, gain experience and acquire new skills. An added benefit is that it helped relieve stress and anxiety that they all felt as children growing up in the civil rights era.

When Francie Mae was a young teenager in the late 1960's, many non-violent activists were worn out due to the constant threats of danger.

In 1967, race riots called "The Long Hot Summer" erupted across the United States. These riots occurred because of racial inequality. Many lives were lost, thousands injured and millions of dollars in property had been destroyed.

Francie Mae learned that President Johnson set up a committee to investigate the race riots. This report was named after its author and called The Kerner Report. After a long study, the conclusion was that social inequality was the cause of riots. It was thought that America is a racist society and was heading toward two societies, one white and one black.

In addition to dealing with racial strife, the Vietnam War was still going on. Many service members returned home physically and mentally injured. Families were torn apart. The enlisted ranks of the military consisted of young people with limited economic opportunities. There seemed to be no end to this unpopular war. There were many protests on college campuses and across the United States to end the war.

A younger group of civil rights activists came into power because they were fed up with the long peaceful demonstrations for equality. They saw that non-violent actions was in-effective against violent whites. This movement was called The Black Power movement and was in force due to perceived failures of the civil rights movement. People were emotional, and tired. There were mandatory curfews in place. Army National Guard Troops were on duty throughout the nation. These activists originated outside of the southern states. Many white people feared these groups of activists with raised black fists and strong voices that shouted "Black Power." There was no reason to fear this group. They were tired of being treated as second class citizens. They demanded that history, art and literature of black people be taught in schools and colleges. Americans need a realistic perspective on the development on the country all races share.

During the 1968 Olympics, two black medalists stood on the podium and raised their black gloved fists as a sign of protest while the national anthem was playing. The Australian medalist on the podium joined them in solidarity. They all wore human rights badges. They were not disrespecting the flag or the national anthem. They were challenging our country to do better. They used their national spotlight to protest against injustices for black people. The United States had remained silent as black people were lynched, bombed, assassinated and hung. They wore black to represent black pride. Most black people were still in poverty, lived in substandard housing, and still struggled to achieve the same rights as white people. The athletes were criticized for their actions. Francie Mae thought it was sad that raised black fists caused fear among some white people. They were the same group of people who thought nothing of the fear, physical acts, and injustices they imposed upon black people.

The new leaders were the black youth of the contemporary generation and were proud of their beautiful black skin. They wanted other black people to feel the same way. Instead of feeling oppressed, they were proud, valued and wanted everyone to appreciate them for who they are. They wanted society to know that black people were also Americans.

The arena of civil rights protests shifted from the south to other regions. Many white people in those regions also wanted their public schools, neighborhoods, unions and corporations to remain white. Black people across the nation were frustrated and riots erupted in non-southern states. The Black Power movement advocated for community control of institutions, organizations and resources. Some black people joined the Nation of Islam. A revolutionary political organization called The Black Panther Party was formed to monitor police brutality and later developed social programs in black communities.

The civil rights movement was not stagnant. The young black activists had different strategies and were more progressive. Like the older civil rights leaders, they shared the same goal of changing behavior and attitudes of white people so everyone will be treated equally.

In October of 1969, the majority of the students participated in a city wide high school boycott called "Black Monday." This boycott was organized by the civil rights leaders in Memphis to protest the all- white school board leading a district that was predominately black. Every Monday, over sixty thousand students and hundreds of teachers were absent from school. Her school had a student leader to keep the students informed. Their leader was a senior who was active in community activities. She was a small fierce girl with a dynamic voice. She wore her hair in a beautiful Afro that reflected black pride. They were in awe of her because of her leadership abilities.

The student leader met with them to review and to make sure they understood the guidance given by the adult civil rights workers. During

Black Monday, some students stayed home and others marched. Francie Mae was one of the marchers. She and her friends lived in a housing project within walking distance of downtown Memphis. They were able to walk and join the other marchers. Her parents understood and supported her need to march. She traded her dancing shoes for marching shoes. She joined in the marches for equality and against injustice. With raised right fists, they shouted Black Power and marched peacefully down the city streets. Their white teenage counterparts did the same.

Thousands of adults and young people lined the streets to support the marchers or to march. With signs held high, they sang and marched peacefully every Monday. In addition to the school demands, the strike also supported striking hospital workers, economic boycott of downtown white businesses and other organizations. White businesses were chosen because many black people patronized downtown businesses due to the close proximity to their homes or bus lines. White business owners collaborated with white politicians and had a voice in the city economics. Their businesses would suffer without the black merchants. This was not only an education fight, it included labor and economics. The boycott ended when some black people were appointed to the school board. Francie Mae and her friends committed themselves to continuing their education so they could be in a better positon to affect change and get out of poverty. This was how they were going to make a difference.

The 1960's was also a time for reform. In addition to the civil rights movement, the women's rights movement was in full swing. Women were no longer satisfied with a lack of professional fulfillment. Francie Mae and her friends were daughters who were coming of age in a man's world. The traditional roles of motherhood and marriage were being challenged. Women exercised greater control over when they would have children and began pursuing careers in traditionally male-dominated fields. More women ran for and won political offices.

It was now in the 1970's and at last graduation day came. Francie Mae was seventeen years old. It was a long journey filled with racial strife, poverty, protests, riots, and hope. She didn't know another life. She graduated in the top ten percent of her large class. She sat on stage wearing the orange gown of her school colors and stared out into the crowd of proud parents, grandparents and others who believed in their children.

She tried to find the faces of her parents but there were too many people. She was comforted in knowing they were in the audience. It was a long struggle but some progress was made.

She decided to go to college to continue her education. She received a partial scholarship but knew she needed more money. She decided to work to earn money and start college the next semester. Even with the partial scholarship and money earned from working, she still didn't have enough money. She applied for financial aid to help pay for her tuition and books. Part of her financial aid included a work study program. She decided to work in the big beautiful library filled with newer books!

In spite of hardships, all five siblings graduated from high school and started their careers. Their parents were proud of them. They were inspired by their parents sacrifice. They provided a solid foundation for all their children in spite of difficult circumstances.

Since the civil rights acts, laws were put in place and progress was made. There is still inequality in society based on society attitudes. There is some element of racism in how society view and judge non-white people and people living in poverty. It is time to stop separating people based on their skin color and economic status. Everyone should help untangle the web so everyone can have equal justice.

Waking Up

Francie Mae eventually woke up from her long nap under the protective oak tree. She couldn't believe she had napped so long! The cool breeze stopped blowing a long time ago. She stood up, brushed the grass from her dress and brushed her long curly hair out of her face. She turned toward the shack and saw her mother watching from the kitchen window. She stretched and looked around for her tattered book. She found it in the nearby brush, grabbed it, and ran toward the shack. She couldn't wait to tell her mother and father about her dream. She had hope for the future!

She had dreamed a glimpse into her future but realized that not much had changed since she was five years old. Some of the laws were changed and the web was untangling. It was a long and painful journey but she didn't quit. There are more strings to untangle. She knew that more people had to help pull on the strings.

Her father was nearly sixty years old when he got his first meaningful job. He served in the Army during World War II. After discharge, because of racist laws, he was denied jobs in favor of white men. He provided for his family the best way he could. He worked many odd jobs without benefits. The south's investment in racism and racist acts caused the web to tangle. Her parents had faith in God, faith in the democratic process, and faith in the goodness of people. They had hope that the heart of man would change and help untangle the web.

While living in shacks, Francie Mae and her siblings were living in a loving home. Their home became their classroom. They had two parents who cared for them, taught them, and answered their questions. They encouraged education and taught them to respect all people. Her parents knew they would make mistakes while growing up. They also knew they would learn from the mistakes and make better choices. They set solid foundations to help them reach their full potential in life. If the foundation is not solid, the rest of the building will collapse.

When laws changed, Francie Mae and her family moved from shacks into a public housing project near downtown Memphis. This was the same housing project she saw from the windows of the city bus four years ago. She was still living in poverty but had stable housing, electricity, indoor plumbing, food assistance and health insurance. This is not enough. Everyone should have basic necessities like food, stable housing, and health insurance. These basic necessities helped bridge the gap from absolute poverty and gave her hope for a successful future.

During her journey, Francie Mae had to go back in history filled with pain to help her understand people and society. Taking the long nap under the oak tree helped her to understand. She knew she was dreaming but her dream was also real life. She struggled to understand systemic racism and racist and classist attitudes that shaped our nation. She struggled to understand why people were oppressed based on skin color and socioeconomic status. She struggled to understand why people in a positon to help were contributors to the problems by remaining silent. Once you understand the why it happens, you can move forward to what you can help do about it.

She traveled a long dark journey to get to the light. Living with racism and poverty was too painful. It was easier to take a nap and dream. She learned that she had an inner strength that would help her continue her fight for justice for all people. It is her hope that the challenges in the past are lessons learned to heal the present and become a beacon of light for the future.

She knew that people have the power to reduce racism and poverty. To do this, they have to change their mindsets and see all people as equals. Everyone has a role to challenge each other to be better. She knew that parents need to start talking to their children about race and poverty. She knew more adults need to speak up if they see racist acts. People need to recognize and eliminate bias against other people. People need to learn the history of other cultures, embrace differences and value diversity. Everyone needs to fight against discriminatory laws. Education will help change the culture and hearts of people.

After eating the simple meal her mother prepared with loving hands, she returned to the big oak tree beside the shack. She felt rain drops fall and lifted her big brown eyes toward the sky. The clouds seemed to be weeping. She ran back to the shack so she wouldn't get drenched. After the sudden rainfall, the sun began shining. She went outside again and saw the beautiful colors in a rainbow. She tried to count the colors. She thought she saw three colors but the longer she looked, she saw more. There was something majestic about seeing these colors working together to bring beauty. She knew the rainbow was God's promise to the world. She chose to focus on the incredible and beautiful life that was promised to her.

The Oak Leaf

A child's mind can be confusing. There is a combination of other factors that makes it almost impossible to discover their own identity. Some of these children grow up with a lot of questions and no answers. If they ask questions and get no answers, the imagination usually takes over and they often come to their own conclusion. They are outsiders within the homes and outsiders in the community. While growing up, Francie Mae and her siblings asked their parents many questions. They tried to provide them with the correct answers. They heard encouraging and uplifting words.

As an adult, Francie Mae knew she was responsible for how she responds to life. The poverty rate is higher in southern states. The majority of the ten poorest states are in the south. This has not changed much over the years. There is still work to be done. It is easier to achieve if everyone had equal rights. She never forgot the civil rights workers who fought tirelessly for equal rights and social justice.

She had to take personal responsibility for what she wanted to do in life. She had the ability overcome a life of poverty. She was expected to make a difference and give back. The ability to give back and serve others gave her joy.

After graduating from high school, Francie Mae went to college in another city and majored in nursing. She registered to vote and voted in her first presidential election. Education provided her with a pathway out of poverty. After graduating from college, she began her professional career.

Many years later, Francie Mae decided to drive and visit the small military town she grew up in. Her family spent six years living there. To her disappointment, "The Bottom" was blocked off and she couldn't drive down the road they walked for many years. Her age of awareness happened while living in this location. It was in this location that they had many conversations around the black pot belly stove. It was in this location that her parents told her they were not poor and taught her about hidden opportunities. It was in this location where she met her first friend. It was in this location that she made promises to the old oak tree. He had listened to her for many years and she wondered if he was still standing.

She turned her car around and drove back to the Navy base. She stopped at the gate and showed her military identification. The young service man smiled and saluted her. She smiled back at him and returned the salute. The gold oak leaf on the collar of her battle dress uniform reminded her of the promise she made to the old oak tree many years ago. She smiled and continued on her way. She was helping to untangle the web.

Untangling the Web

Social awareness

- ◊ Notice indicators of possible problems earlier
- ◊ Be a bit more open minded
- ◊ Be more confident
- ◊ Have a bit more control
- ◊ Be better at accepting different groups in society
- ◊ Improve my communication
- ◊ Respect others
- ◊ Be friendly
- ◊ Help others
- ◊ Not judge others
- ◊ Be more responsible
- ◊ Know what is happening before dealing with problems
- ◊ Think before I speak
- ◊ Believe in myself
- ◊ Fix the little things
- ◊ Be more willing to try new things
- ◊ Be a contributor using my strengths
- ◊ Ask if others are okay
- ◊ Know my own value
- ◊ Help at home

Francie Mae and her siblings had loving parents. In spite of living in poverty, they were healthy, happy and did not have a poverty mindset. They did not believe they would live in poverty forever. The tangled web was full of negative attitudes that other people believed. They didn't believe the same way.

Her parents provided guidance and support. They encouraged them to talk about their concerns and provided answers to their many questions. They clung onto hope. Now that she knew why people were treated differently, she knew what she had to do to help make changes. She encouraged her friends and other people to make changes. They pulled at the strings of the tangled web together.

Her parents knew things would get better. Laws would be changed and all people would have equal rights. They also knew that some people would not feel the same way. They would continue to hold onto beliefs that are hidden in the tangled web. They hoped that eventually, those people would get tired of their beliefs and work on untangling the web.

Francie Mae learned that freedom is not free and should not be taken for granted. In 1968, Dr. King came to her hometown of Memphis, Tennessee to protest the dangerous working conditions of the black garbage workers. Dr. King was shot and killed while standing on the balcony of the Lorraine Motel. This was a day that the whole world seemed to stand still. She was now old enough to understand the reasons behind poverty and the struggle for equality.

As a teenager, Francie Mae remembered her promises and participated in marches to fight for justice. When she was old enough, she exercised her right to vote. Like Cousin Fessor, she went to college and chose to work in a career she loved.

When she was a little girl living in poverty, she was a dreamer. She learned to be tenacious. She had an industrious spirit that was waiting to be released. As a poor family living in poverty, the odds were stacked against them. Her parents didn't believe in odds. They didn't have much money but taught them to be strong and resilient. Because of them, even in poverty, she learned not to invest in things that depreciate. It's important to invest in things that appreciate over time. Her parents invested in their children and they profited from each stage of their lives.

Her parents taught them not to have a poverty mentality. They didn't allow their present circumstances to define their future. They taught her to look for hidden opportunities. She opened her eyes and found these opportunities were within her sight. She just had to know where to look. In spite of the odds of a poor girl graduating from high school, she graduated with honors, and later graduated from college

She and her siblings made it out of poverty by having encouraging parents, knowing their rights, having a positive outlook, being good citizens, and getting an education. They were strong and powerful like the eagle soaring through the sky. Webs are tangled like a ball of yarn. It takes patience and creativity to untangle them. Sometimes it takes a long time but it was worth the effort to get out of poverty and stay out of poverty. They tried to keep the string from getting tangled again. To overcome poverty and racism, it's easier if everyone grabs a string and pull.

After telling her dream to her parents, Francie Mae was comforted. It helped her to talk about her inner most feelings. It helps to have loving parents to explain what she was too young to understand. She had to learn how to stand up to bullies, endure racism and poverty. In spite of her struggles, she didn't lose focus on her short and long term goals. She gained strength, became resilient, and prevailed over poverty!

Something to Look Forward To

Live your best life! You can choose to succeed in whatever you were meant to be while uplifting others. There are many opportunities in life that should be shared. Everyone has a history. Good or bad, it's our story. Having knowledge of history helps us to understand what our ancestors endured, understand other people and ourselves. We learn and grow from past mistakes but shouldn't repeat them. When we know better, we should do better. We are now living in the gift of the present and should look forward to an amazing future.

I lived in poverty and with racism my entire childhood. I grew up during the civil rights era and lived with protests, riots and other violence on an almost daily basis. Children were too young to process what was going on. In some instances, children who participated in the protests were hosed with water and yelled at. Children lost their lives when a church was bombed. How do you talk with children about this? Parents didn't understand what was happening and didn't know how to explain these occurrences to their children. How do you make sense out of something that was senseless? It was a hard conversation to have but necessary so children wouldn't form their own conclusions. My parents had many conversations with my siblings and me. Many of our conversations occurred when we sat around a pot belly stove in the middle of our shack. This was our safe place.

Along with many others, I survived those dark years and became a productive member of society. The purpose of this book is to provide insight into the plight of minorities and the poor. It's past time for society to hold on to unfounded stereotypes. Minorities and poor people are not invisible. The voice of those struggling with racism and poverty must be understood. We must use our voice to help change the atmosphere.

People still living in poverty should be empowered to know there is a way out and make better choices. Everyone should be treated equally. As we journey through life we must understand, respect, support and learn from each other.

Be a part of the ongoing fight for justice for everyone. Since the civil rights acts, progress has been made but there is still inequality in our society based on society attitudes, laws that should be overhauled, and personal mindsets. There is some element of racism in how society view minorities and judge people living in poverty.

When we understand systemic issues and history affecting minorities and the poor, we can make individual decisions to affect change. Once we understand the why, we can move forward. When we affect change, we make a difference. Let's focus on what we can change. We can continue to fight for equality, vote to overhaul laws, and change our mindset and mentality relating to racism and poverty.

God made us all in His image. We are to form relationships with Him and each other. The first commandment is to love Him and the second is to love our neighbors as thyself. We are our brother's keepers. During my journey, I had many mentors to help me (friends, relatives, teachers, pastors, co-workers, and the list goes on). If you can change the hearts of people, you can change the culture.

I am sharing my story as a living testimony to help and empower others. We can get out of the wilderness of poverty. It is not a solo journey. God has people strategically placed to help as we travel across rough terrains of life. We can brave elements we never thought we could. We can climb over obstacles too high for our short legs. We can declutter our life and mind from unhealthy cobwebs of despair. Doors will shut in our face and windows will open.

We will fail according to the world's standards. Those same failures will be success according to God's standards. Failures will become our strength and help us grow. People will disappoint us but we should never disappoint our self. Part of living is dying. We have to let some things die. Let racism, inequality, bullying and negativity die.

We can do better! It is time to break the generational curse of poverty! Poverty has claimed too many families and left them feeling hopeless like strangers in our own land. Poverty transcends economics. Many people have a poverty mindset or mentality. This prevents people from investing in them and limits their success. We must keep our head up and focus on our goals. We have to want to live a good life, believe it, and fight for it. This involves changing our mindset and educating others to change their mindset.

Over the years, I learned the difference between happiness and joy. Happiness is an emotion in which we experience a wide range of feelings. It may be temporary and may be caused by earthly experiences or material objects. Joy is a stronger and less common feeling than happiness. It may be caused by spiritual experiences, caring for others, gratitude and thankfulness. As a result of my trials and tribulations, I now have daily joy.

Structural factors such as racism, gender-based discrimination and economic inequality continue to exist. Bias against the poor and people of color lead to unfair practices and people were victims of the criminal justice system. Life is not equal for all Americans. Many people joined the civil rights workers and fought against unjust laws that prevented progress. Federal laws were passed but ignored by southern states and not enforced. Some laws are in need of reform. Most people want a hand up, not a hand out. Safety net programs are stepping stones to a better lifestyle. People rely on these programs for basic necessities. Recognize them for their intent.

As a member of a group that was discriminated against, affirmative action provided access to education, housing, employment and discrimination in the workplace. It helped to level the playing field so everyone can get to the starting line. We were affected by structural factors but instead of breaking under pressure, God gave us strength. As a result of the fight for equality, and subsequent laws, we had a chance to succeed.

We've all been through and will continue to go through difficult times. Some children living in poverty may experience physical or psychological barriers. Long term stressors may result in anger or rage. Children may act out and engage in unhealthy behaviors. These children grow up, become adults, and may repeat the cycle. I experienced rage when I was bullied as a child. I experienced anger while living environment that was different from my peers. Living in a society that judges us based on our skin color or economic status is tough. I was determined to live a better life. My pathway out of poverty started as a child.

My siblings and I were fortunate to have good parents that supported and encouraged us. Our parents knew when we were struggling to make sense of the world we were living in. As a family, we had many conversations about racism and poverty. We learned many life skills. They sought healthy outlets to help us release our stress. They told and showed us we were loved. They taught us how to respect others. They taught us to never discriminate. They took us to church and taught us about faith and hope. They taught us how to live a Christian life. They taught us the importance of being good citizens and explained to us why we should vote. Even though we were poor, we gave back by volunteering. They served as model examples for us to see and imitate.

I encourage parents to talk with their children about these ongoing and difficult problems affecting our country. I've included some tips of engagement I learned as a child. These suggestions are not inclusive but I hope they are a starting point to have honest conversations.

1. Children see and recognize color. No one is colorblind. Don't remain silent. It's okay to talk about race. Have age appropriate conversations. Explain why we are different and focus on how we are more alike. The same color is boring. We are different colors for a reason.

2. Children learn what they live. Sometimes people may not realize their actions and behaviors are racist. Hidden racism is still racism. Model your behavior to be a positive example for children. Share honest opinions. Acknowledge your feelings and their feelings.

Allow children to ask questions and encourage them to share theirs. Speak out against racism.

3. Explain racism, prejudice and bias and how it impacts other people. Racism is learned and poverty is man-made. Explain why laws were put in place so everyone would have equal rights. Explain that people should be held accountable for laws that are in place. Be honest. If you don't know the answer to some questions, it's okay but try to find the answer. We live in the age of information. This information is available on the internet and in books. Read for awareness and understanding. Read books written by minority authors. Don't be judgmental. Understand why government programs are in place to help low income people. Practice living on a low income budget for a month.

4. Explain systemic racism and how it affects other people. Systemic or institutional racism is a form of racism that is expressed in the practice of social and political institutions. It may result in disparities in healthcare, wealth, income, criminal justice, employment, housing and other factors. Explain that some people are unfairly targeted based on their skin color. Explain that some practices and policies are in place that harm some racial groups and help others. Vote in all elections. Vote for policies and laws that benefit all people and hold politicians accountable.

5. Express anger appropriately. Anger is a normal reaction but shouldn't be directed toward people based on race or socio-economic status. Learn how to problem solve and channel negative energy into positive energy. If children are angry because of events out of their control, help them identify healthy ways to express their anger. Encourage reading, journaling, athletic activities, church activities or volunteering. Join bridge building organizations to learn about how to be part of the solution.

6. Assess fear. Talk about racist encounters and how to respond. Children watch what you do and don't do. Teach children not to fear others because of their skin color or socio-economic status. Make friends with people of different races and socio-economic status and encourage your children to do the same. Explain that bullying is wrong and explain how it affects other

people. Sometimes the bullies are the one's hurting and they don't know healthy ways to release their emotions. Other people may be bullied because of their skin color, feelings of powerlessness, academic accomplishments or socioeconomic status. Speak up and tell someone if you are bullied or see someone bullied. Talk to your children and teach them right and wrong.

7. Teach and embrace cultural diversity. Get to know neighbors and people in the community of different races. Attend predominately minority church services. Participate in cultural activities of other races. Be the model you want your children to emulate.

8. Provide hope and reassurance. Comfort your children and teach them that there are many people who are working to make things better for all people. There are people who want justice and equality for everyone. Choose to focus on these people. Have trusted mentors and become a trusted mentor to others.

9. Learn the value of friendship. Friendship is not based on the "haves" and "have nots" or skin color. It is a mutual affection between people. Sometimes friendships dissolve because interests and opinions change. Let your children know that it's okay to end friendships that may be hurtful. Find friends who fit into a better future for everyone.

10. Empower your children to be change agents. Teach and talk with your children about the roles and responsibilities of police, law enforcement officers and politicians. Most police officers and law enforcement officers have high ethical standards. These professionals are the face of the public and are in a position of trust. Hold them accountable to protect and serve all people. Teach and talk with your children about their roles and responsibilities as citizens. Everyone can affect change.

Life is a journey of discovery. It was not meant to be traveled alone. It's not about us, it's about others. We need to start looking at people as individuals, not as labels. The heart must change so the culture can change. Living a quality life involves taking responsibility and being a change agent for the good of everyone.

Other people helped my family and me survive and eventually thrive while living with racism and in poverty. People were willing to fight for equal justice and social equality. People were willing to change their mindsets so they could understand the plight of others and fight to make our great nation better for everyone. They were change agents.

Even while living poverty; my goal was to get out and remain out. It was my responsibility to take the long road out. It was important for me to know my history and my truth. I learned that a few people can negatively or positively influence a large number of people. I had to learn to choose to look for positive influencers and later become a positive influencer. I had to put the right people in my wisdom circle. We all have a past; we remember it, learn from it but don't live in it. The truth cleanses the soul and opens up space for new adventures. We have a past story and a future story!

We should leave a legacy of equal justice and social equality for future generations. We can all pull strings to help untangle the old outdated web!

About the Author

Frances Hewlett Morris was born in Memphis, Tennessee. She grew up in absolute poverty during the Civil Rights Era. As a child, her first job was working long hours in the cotton fields for low wages. She is a graduate of Tennessee State University. She started her professional career as a registered nurse at a teaching hospital dedicated to serving the under-served population.

She continued to grow professionally and began researching why the poverty cycle exists. As an advocate for justice, she continued her studies and earned a Master's degree in Health Law. She is a retired military officer and health care leader for a Fortune 500 company. She used her voice to help empower people and implemented programs to promote better health outcomes. She had the opportunity to engage with a diverse group of people and learn about different life experiences.

She took a journey through a land showing the dark-side while searching for her piece of the American dream. She was economically poor but didn't have a poverty mentality. Her parents taught their children how to survive and thrive in spite of their humble beginnings.

Faith, family and fun are important to her. She is a mother, grandmother, sibling and widow. She loves to laugh out loud, dance lively and enjoy life's adventures. She believes we all have a future story that can be powerful and joyful when the right seeds are planted.

She decided to share her intimate, powerful and inspiring memoir to help empower others to understand why poverty exists and how to escape its powerful clutches. In her blog, Francie Mae's Journey, she shared part of her life in poverty, her pathways to success and how to prevail over poverty. Her goal is to help find common ground, and empower others to break the shackles of poverty.

www.franciemae.com